Puchta · Stranks · Lewis-Jones

MORE! ①
GRAMMAR PRACTICE

HELBLING
LANGUAGES

Mit Bescheid vom 12. November 2009, GZ: BMUKK-5.001/0030-V/9/2009, hat das Bundesministerium für Unterricht, Kunst und Kultur das Unterrichtsmittel „MORE! Grammar Practice 1" von Puchta u.a. antragsgemäß in der vorliegenden Fassung gemäß §14 Abs. 2 und 5 des Schulunterrichtsgesetzes, BGBl. Nr. 472/86 und gemäß den derzeit geltenden Lehrplänen als für den Unterrichtsgebrauch an Hauptschulen und an allgemein bildenden höheren Schulen für die Klasse 1 im Unterrichtsgegenstand Englisch (1. lebende Fremdsprache) geeignet erklärt.

MORE! 1 GRAMMAR PRACTICE

by
Herbert Puchta
Jeff Stranks
Peter Lewis-Jones

© Helbling Languages 2010

www.helblinglanguages.com

Design and layout by Amanda Hockin

Illustrated by Roberto Battestini, Giovanni Giorgi Pierfranceschi, Lorenzo Sabbatini, Nicola Zanni

Printed by Athesia

First published 2010

Second edition 2012, third print run

ISBN 978-3-85272-223-8

Schulbuchnummer: 146.076

Contents

Introduction

Liebe Schülerin!
Lieber Schüler!

Wenn du Sport betreibst, ist es für dich selbstverständlich, dass du regelmäßig trainierst. Wer im Schwimmen, beim Laufen, im Fußball oder beim Tischtennis seine Leistung verbessern will, merkt bald, dass regelmäßiges Üben zu besseren Resultaten führt. Aber nicht nur das — wer mehrfach wöchentlich trainiert, hat auch mehr Spaß am Üben, und was zuerst vielleicht etwas mühsam erscheint, gelingt bald viel besser und fast mühelos.

Mit dem Grammatiküben ist das nicht anders. Wer regelmäßig übt, macht bald weniger Fehler, erzielt bessere Ergebnisse und hat außerdem mehr Spaß an der Sprache. Die Übungen in diesem Buch und auf der beiliegenden CD-ROM sind so gebaut, dass sie garantiert bessere Lernleistungen bringen, wenn du sie regelmäßig durchführst. Also, am besten nicht etwa kurz vor einem Test ein paar Stunden üben! Du wirst bessere Resultate erzielen, wenn du dich mehrfach wöchentlich mit Grammatik beschäftigst. Dann brauchst du auch nicht so lange zu üben. Wie wär's mit 10 Minuten vier mal pro Woche? Versuch's mal — die ersten positiven Resultate werden sich einstellen!

Im Buch und auf der CD-ROM findest du die folgenden Hilfen:

- Das Inhaltsverzeichnis — zum schnellen Auffinden des Grammatikkapitels, das du üben möchtest.

- Jedes Grammatikkapitel beginnt mit einer Zusammenfassung der wichtigsten Formen und Regeln.

- Neben der Zusammenfassung findest du meist eine Ankündigung von Professor Grammar. Wenn du dieses Symbol siehst, solltest du am besten gleich mal in die CD-ROM schauen.

- Professor Grammar wird dir auf der CD-ROM im Abschnitt *How it works* helfen, eine Struktur besser zu verstehen. Im Bereich *Check it out* kannst du dann gleich mal versuchen, ob du die Erklärungen richtig verstanden hast.

- Nun kannst du wählen, ob du mit Hilfe der CD-ROM weiterüben möchtest, oder zuerst mit dem Buch arbeitest. Auf der CD-ROM findest du zu jedem Grammatikkapitel zwei oder drei Übungen, zum Beispiel Sätze mit Lücken, in die du die richtige Form einsetzen musst. Du kannst hier wählen, ob du dir zuerst die richtigen Lösungen anhören möchtest (*Listen*), und dann die Übung machen willst, oder ob du zuerst die Übung versuchen willst um sie dir vielleicht anschließend anzuhören.

- Im Buch selbst findest du zu jedem Grammatikkapitel eine oder mehrere Seiten an Übungen. Sie sind so angeordnet, dass du zuerst leichtere Übungen vorfindest und der Schwierigkeitsgrad allmählich gesteigert wird.

- Im Anhang zum Buch findest du eine Zusammenstellung aller Grammatikkapitel, die im Buch behandelt werden, mit Schautafeln, die dir eine gute Übersicht geben und den wichtigsten Regeln. Falls du mal ein Wort nicht kennen solltest, kannst du es in der Wordlist im Anhang nachschlagen. Außerdem findest du im Anhang auch die Lösungen — die solltest du dir am besten immer dann anschauen, wenn du deine Leistungen überprüfen möchtest, oder dich bei einem Kapitel mal gar nicht auskennst. Was wenig Sinn macht ist das regelmäßige Ansehen der Lösungen, bevor du eine Übung machst. Aber das weißt du ja selbst und auch hier gilt, was im Training im Sport gilt: Wer schummelt, beschummelt sich selbst.

- Und nun noch ein Tipp zum Schluss: auf der CD-ROM findest du zu jedem Grammatikkapitel einen *Cartoon* mit einem lustigen Rätsel.

- Ja, und dann hat Professor Grammar sich auch gelegentlich Tricks ausgedacht, um dir besonderen Lernspaß zu bereiten! Aber nun geht's los.

Viel Spaß und viel Erfolg wünschen dir die Autoren!

Herbert Puchta
Jeff Stranks
Peter Lewis-Jones

Plural nouns — irregular plurals

Hello! See me on the CD-ROM to discover more about *plural nouns* and *irregular plurals* and to learn better when to use them.

Plural nouns

Die Mehrzahl zu bilden ist im Englischen normalerweise einfach: du hängst an die Einzahl ein **-s** an.
Wenn ein Wort mit **-y** endet, vor dem ein Mitlaut steht, musst du die Mehrzahl mit **-ies** bilden.

a dog – 4 dog**s**

a snake – 7 snake**s**

a baby – 8 bab**ies**

Irregular plurals

Es gibt einige Ausnahmen! Die lernst du am besten mit jedem neuen Wort gleich mit.

a child – two **children**

a fish – three **fish**

a mouse – two **mice**

a foot – two **feet**

I Match.

1 a frog	**4** a baby	**7** a gorilla	**10** eight bananas
2 five frogs	**5** three babies	**8** a banana	**11** a snake
3 two frogs	**6** four gorillas	**9** five bananas	**12** six snakes

2 Write the words.

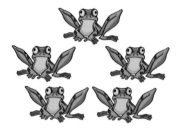

1 .... *a snake* ....   2 .... *three snakes* ....   3 ....   4 ....

5 ....   6 ....   7 ....   8 ....

9 ....   10 ....   11 ....   12 ....

13 ....   14 ....   15 ....   16 ....

3 Write the plural nouns.

1 Do you like .... *dogs* .... ? (dog)

2 I don't like .... very much. (pony)

3 There are two .... in the garden. (cat)

4 My mother's friend has got three .... ! (baby)

5 Let's go to the pet shop and buy two white .... ! (mouse)

6 I've got two .... in a cage in my room. (hamster)

7 My pet bat eats .... (insect)

8 My dad's got really big .... ! (foot)

9 My friend Jim has got four blue-and-yellow .... in a tank. (fish)

10 My aunt and uncle have got three .... (child)

And now go to the CD-ROM and do the *Cartoon for Fun!*

Imperatives

So sagst du, was jemand tun oder nicht tun soll.

+	-
Sit down.	**Don't sit** down.
Put your books in your bag.	**Don't put** your books in your bag.
Run!	**Don't run**!

1 **Write the sentences in the speech bubbles.**

Don't clean the board.   Don't open the window.   Run!   Sh. Don't speak.
Open your bag, please.   Don't eat the banana.   Look at me.   Sit down, please.

2 **Make the sentences negative.**

1 Open the window.

....

2 Walk.

....

3 Close your books.

....

4 Stand up.

....

5 Look at the picture.

....

6 Tell me your name.

....

7 Speak.

....

8 Eat your apple.

....

3 **Put the words in order.**

1 door / the / close

....

2 open / don't / books / your

....

3 me / at / look / don't

....

4 your / me / name / tell

....

5 your / out / books / take

....

6 don't / window / the / clean

....

7 my / eat / ice cream / don't

....

8 pen / bag / put / in / your / your

....

4 **Complete the sentences with the words in the box.**

down	the window
your name	my chocolate
books	green
up	at me

1 Stand ....

2 Sit ....

3 Don't eat ....

4 Don't tell me ....

5 Don't look ....

6 Close ....

7 Don't open your ....

8 Colour the grass ....

5 **Look at the pictures and write the sentences.**

1 ....

2 ....

3 ....

4 ....

5 ....

6 ....

7 ....

8 ....

And now go to the CD-ROM and do the *Cartoon for Fun!*

to be (affirmative)

Hello! See me on the CD-ROM to discover more about *to be (affirmative)* and to learn better when to use it.

Das Verb **to be** kommt mit folgenden Formen im Englischen sehr oft vor.

I**'m** (= I **am**) tired.	You**'re** (= You **are**) clever.	He**'s** (= He **is**) nice.
	We**'re** (= We **are**) busy.	She**'s** (= She **is**) in class 3B.
	They**'re** (= They **are**) twelve.	It**'s** (= It **is**) blue.

Du kannst die Formen von **to be** in der Langform (**I am**) oder der Kurzform (**I'm**) schreiben.
Beim Sprechen verwendest du fast immer die Kurzform.

1 Write the phrases in the bubbles.

He's tired.   ~~It's green.~~
She's tired.   They're green.
I'm busy.   We're twelve.
They're busy.   They're twelve.

It's green.

2 Write *am / are / is.*

1 I ...*am*.... tired.

2 She .... lovely.

3 The pen .... new.

4 You .... clever!

5 The books .... old.

6 The teacher .... tired.

7 The children .... busy.

8 The new shoes .... lovely.

And now go to the CD-ROM and do the *Cartoon for Fun!*

Prepositions (*in, on, under, next to*)

Das sind nützliche kleine Wörter, die dir sagen, wo sich etwas befindet.

Hello! See me on the CD-ROM to discover more about *prepositions* and to learn better when to use them.

1 Mark T (*True*) or F (*False*).

1 The rabbit's in the box. `F`

2 The frogs are next to the television. ☐

3 The cat's under the chair. ☐

4 The books are on the table. ☐

5 The dog's next to the cat. ☐

6 The banana's on the television. ☐

7 The snake's in the table. ☐

8 The children are on the table. ☐

2 Write *in / on / under / next to*.

1 The frog's ......*on*...... the bicycle.

2 The frog's .... the crocodile.

3 The cat's .... the ball.

4 The cat's .... the fridge.

5 The banana's .... the gorilla.

6 The rabbit's .... the hat.

7 The snake's .... the gorilla.

8 The dogs are .... the table.

And now go to the CD-ROM and do the *Cartoon for Fun!*

there is / there are

Hello! See me on the CD-ROM to discover more about *there is / there are* and to learn better when to use them.

Mit **there is / there are** drückst du aus, dass etwas da ist oder es etwas gibt.

There**'s a** monster in the tree. (= There is a monster in the tree.)

There **are** three frog**s** on the table.

1 **Match the pictures and sentences.**

1 There's a crocodile in the room.
2 There are crocodiles in the room.
3 There's a snake on the bed.
4 There are snakes on the bed.

5 There's a rabbit next to the car.
6 There are rabbits next to the car.
7 There's a monster under the bed.
8 There are monsters under the bed.

2 **Complete with *'s* or *are*.**

1 There ......*are*...... two cats on the bed.
2 There .... a laptop on the chair.
3 There .... a pizza on the table.
4 There .... six monkeys in the tree.
5 There .... a frog in the grass.

6 There .... twenty children in the classroom.
7 There .... an insect in my school bag.
8 There .... fish in the pool.

3 Use words from the boxes to write the sentences.

	a dog		the car.
	two dogs	in	the bed.
There is	a gorilla	on	the fridge.
There are	four gorillas	under	the chair.
	a bear	next to	the table.
	three bears		the bag.

1 There are two dogs on the table.
2 ....
3 ....
4 ....
5 ....
6 ....

4 Complete the dialogues.

1 A Don't eat the ice cream!
   B Why?
   A There's an insect in .... it.

2 A Don't close your book!
   B Why?
   A ....
       .... on it.

3 A Be quiet!
   B Why?
   A ....
       .... bed.

4 A Run!
   B Why?
   A ....
       ....
   the classroom!

5 A Don't sit down!
   B Why?
   A ....
       ....
   the chair.

6 A Close the door!
   B Why?
   A ....
       .... outside*.

*****outside** — draußen, vor der Türe

And now go to the CD-ROM and do the *Cartoon for Fun!*

have got – haven't got

Hello! See me on the CD-ROM to discover more about *have got / haven't got* and to learn better when to use them.

Du verwendest **have got / haven't got**, wenn du sagen möchtest, dass jemand etwas hat oder nicht hat, oder fragen willst, ob er/sie etwas hat. Wenn du es schreibst, kannst du die Langform oder die Kurzform verwenden.

+	–	?
I've got (= I **have got**)	I **haven't got** (= I **have not got**)	Have I got ...?
You've got (= You **have got**)	You **haven't got** (= You **have not got**)	Have you got ...?
He's got (= He **has got**)	He **hasn't got** (= He **has not got**)	Has he got ...?
She's got (= She **has got**)	She **hasn't got** (= She **has not got**)	Has she got ...?
It's got (= It **has got**)	It **hasn't got** (= It **has not got**)	Has it got ...?
We've got (= We **have got**)	We **haven't got** (= We **have not got**)	Have we got ...?
You've got (= You **have got**)	You **haven't got** (= You **have not got**)	Have you got ...?
They've got (= They **have got**)	They **haven't got** (= They **have not got**)	Have they got ...?

1 Read the sentences and look at the pictures. Write **T** (*True*) or **F** (*False*).

1 He's got big feet. ☐ T

2 He's got a small nose. ☐

3 He's got a bike. ☐

4 He hasn't got a wooden leg. ☐

5 She's got a laptop. ☐

6 They haven't got big ears. ☐

7 She's got long black hair. ☐

8 They've all got a parrot on their shoulder. ☐

2 Read the sentences. Write the names of the girls under the pictures.

 CD-ROM

 ①

 ②

 ③

 ④

....

Annabel hasn't got long hair.   Annabel hasn't got a big nose.   Annabel hasn't got big ears.

Louise has got long hair.   Louise hasn't got a big nose.   Louise has got big ears.

Maggie's got long hair.   Maggie hasn't got a big nose.   Maggie hasn't got big ears.

Susan's got short hair.   Susan's got a big nose.   Susan's got big ears.

3 Write the words in the correct order.

1 new / We've / a / got / car
We've got a new car.

2 eyes / mother / got / My / blue / has
....

3 six / I / got / brothers and sisters / have
....

4 got / A / legs / snake / hasn't
....

5 We / haven't / got / tonight / homework
....

6 family / got / a / hasn't / My / dog
....

4 Make the sentences negative.

1 I've got long hair.
I haven't got long hair.

2 They've got green eyes.
....

3 My father's got a big car.
....

4 She's got a new laptop.
....

5 I've got homework this weekend.
....

6 We've got a dog.
....

5 Complete the questions and answers. Use short forms when you can.

1 **A** ...*Have*... you ......*got*... a cat?
   B No, but I've got a dog!

2 **A** .... your brother .... a big nose?
   B No, but he .... big ears!

3 **A** .... your parents .... a car?
   B Yes, and my sister .... a car, too.

4 **A** .... your classroom .... a computer?
   B No, but the school .... a special computer room.

5 **A** .... you .... a laptop?
   B No, I .... !

6 Write the correct form of *have got* in each space. (✓ = positive, ✗ = negative)

My friends

I [1] *'ve got* .... (✓) lots of friends. My best friend, Sean, [2] .... (✓) long hair and green eyes – he's cool! He [3] .... (✓) three dogs at home – we go there after school and play with them. One dog [4] .... (✗) a tail!*

Julia's my friend, too. She lives in my street. Her father [5] .... (✓) a lot of money and her house is really big – it [6] .... (✓) six bedrooms! But it [7] .... (✗) a swimming pool – it's a shame* because Julia likes swimming. But we [8] .... (✓) a pool at our school so Julia swims there.

Julia's brother Andy is my friend too. He likes animals – he [9] .... (✓) a parrot in his bedroom! (He [10] .... (✓) a snake too – and I don't like snakes!) But Julia and Andy [11] .... (✗) a dog or a cat – I don't know why not.

tail – Schwanz   *it's a shame* – das ist schade

And now go to the CD-ROM and do the *Cartoon for Fun!*

14

to be (negative)

Hello! See me on the CD-ROM to discover more about *to be (negative)* and to learn better when to use it.

So wird das Verb **to be** verneint:

I'm not nervous. (= I am not ...)
You/We/They **aren't** happy. (= You/We/They are not ...)
He/She **isn't** bored. (= He/She is not ...)

1 Complete with the words in the box.

hot	grey
morning	small
~~English~~	wrong

1 Leona Lewis isn't American. She's ....English.......... .
2 Elephants aren't blue. They're ....
3 3 + 8 = 12. That isn't right. It's ....
4 Brazil isn't a cold country. It's ....

5 Breakfast isn't in the afternoon. It's in the ....
6 Hamsters aren't big. They're quite ....

2 Look at the pictures and tick the correct sentences.

1 ☐ Today isn't Wednesday.
☐ Today isn't Tuesday.

2 ☐ The cat isn't on the chair.
☐ The cat isn't under the chair.

3 ☐ Charlotte isn't happy.
☐ Charlotte isn't angry.

4 ☐ The pens aren't next to the book.
☐ The pens aren't on the book.

5 ☐ It isn't night.
☐ It isn't morning.

6 ☐ The frog isn't in the crocodile.
☐ The frog isn't on the crocodile.

3 Write the short forms.

1 She is not Italian.
She isn't Italian.

2 They are not happy.
....

3 I am not bored.
....

4 We are not cold.
....

4 Make the sentences negative. Use short forms.

1 I am English. ....*I'm not English.*.........
2 You are 15. ....
3 They are French. ....

4 He is happy. ....
5 We are from Genova. ....
6 It is blue. ....

5 **Complete the dialogue.**

Lucy Hello Zack.

Jeb I [1] ...'m not... Zack. I'm Jeb.

Lucy Oh sorry. But you are in class 3B.

Jeb No, I [2] .... in 3B. I'm in 3A.

Lucy Oh. But Dave and Fred are your best friends.

Jeb No, Fred and Dave [3] .... my best friends. Carlos is.

Lucy Carlos? Oh Carlos, the boy from France.

Jeb Carlos [4] .... French. He's Spanish.

Lucy Oh, I'm sorry. I'm very tired today.

Jeb You [5] .... tired. You're confused*. Zack and I are twins*.

Lucy Twins!

confused – verwirrt *twins* – Zwillinge

6 **Follow the lines. Tick T (True) or F (False). Correct the false sentences.**

		T	F
1	Kevin's a lion.	✓	
2	Peter and Paul are pelicans.		✓
	Peter and Paul aren't pelicans. They're owls.		
3	Lumpy's a hippo.		
	....		
4	Henry's an elephant.		
	....		
5	David and Victoria are mice.		
	....		
6	Kate and Andre are hamsters.		
	....		
7	Daisy's an owl.		
	....		
8	Rio's a mouse.		
	....		
9	Gordon's a gorilla.		
	....		

David and Victoria   Gordon   Rio   Daisy   Henry   Kevin   Kate and Andre   Peter and Paul   Lumpy

7 **Read about Dylan. How different are you? Write sentences about you.**

All about Dylan	All about me
I'm 13.	I'm not 13, I'm 12. / I'm 13 too.
I'm from England.	....
My hair's black.	....
My eyes are blue.	....
My favourite day is Monday.	....
My favourite animals are hippos.	....
My favourite food is salad.	....
My best friend is called Tom.	....

Hi, I'm Dylan.

CD-ROM

And now go to the CD-ROM and do the *Cartoon for Fun!*

Questions with *be*

Hello! See me on the CD-ROM to discover more about *questions with be* and to learn better when to use them.

Question	Short answer
Am I right?	**Yes, you are. / No,** you're **not.**
Are you happy?	**Yes**, I **am. / No,** I'm **not.**
Is Ben/Sally nervous?	**Yes,** he/she **is. / No,** he/she **isn't.**
Are Fred and Dan American?	**Yes,** they **are. / No,** they **aren't.**

1 Look at the pictures and tick the correct answer for each question.

1 Is Ralph happy?
- ☐ Yes, he is.
- ☑ No, he isn't.

2 Is Yasmin tired?
- ☐ Yes, she is.
- ☐ No, she isn't.

3 Is the car new?
- ☐ Yes, it is.
- ☐ No, it isn't.

4 Are the dogs clever?
- ☐ Yes, they are.
- ☐ No, they aren't.

5 Are we late?
- ☐ Yes, you are.
- ☐ No, you aren't.

6 Are you hot?
- ☐ Yes, I am.
- ☐ No, I'm not.

2 Choose the correct options.

1 <u>Are</u> / Is your eyes green?
2 Am / Is I late?
3 Is / Are we right?
4 Am / Is it cold today?
5 Are / Am they American?
6 Is / Are Dana nervous?
7 Are / Am George and Tom in the classroom?
8 Am / Is it Tuesday tomorrow?

3 Complete the dialogues with the missing words.

1 A .....*Is*.... it her birthday?
   B Yes, it is.

2 A .... you angry?
   B Yes, I ....

3 A .... your computer new?
   B No, it ....

4 A .... I wrong?
   B Yes, you ....

5 A .... the children hungry?
   B No, they ....

6 A .... we late?
   B Yes, we ....

7 A .... Carl scared?
   B No, he ....

8 A .... Jane your friend?
   B Yes, she ....

4 **Put the words in order to make questions.**

1 today / are / 12 / you / ?

....

2 late / I / school / for / am / ?

....

3 eyes / your / blue / are / ?

....

4 your / Julia / friend / best / is / ?

....

5 book / the / is / under / table / the / ?

....

6 Dave / is / Australia / from / ?

....

7 weekend / we / this / busy / are / ?

....

5 **Match the answers to the questions in ④.**

1 ☐6☐ No, he isn't. **3** ☐ No, I'm not. **5** ☐ Yes, we are. **7** ☐ Yes, it is.

2 ☐ No, they're not. **4** ☐ Yes, you are. **6** ☐ Yes, she is.

6 **Look at the picture and answer the questions.**

1 Is the teacher happy?
No, he isn't.

2 Is the big mouse on his head?

....

....

3 Is the big mouse on his shoulder?

....

4 Are the small mice under the table?

....

5 Are the small mice in the box?

....

6 Is the box on the floor?

....

7 Are the students nervous?

....

8 Is the day Thursday?

....

7 **Answer the questions about yourself.**

1 Are you 12?
Yes I am. / No, I'm not.

2 Is blue your favourite colour?

....

3 Are horses your favourite animals?

....

4 Are you Italian?

....

5 Is it Thursday today?

....

6 Are you hungry?

....

7 Is football your favourite sport?

....

8 Are you happy today?

....

And now go to the CD-ROM and do the *Cartoon for Fun!*

Possessives

Hello! See me on the CD-ROM to discover more about *possessives* and to learn better when to use them.

So sagst du, dass dir oder jemandem etwas gehört, oder etwas zu dir oder jemandem gehört.

Dawn is **my/your/her/his/our/their** sister.

I'm the singer in a band. **Its** name is Be Bop.

1 Underline the correct word.

What's you / <u>your</u> favourite band?

Elastic are ¹ I / my favourite band. ² I / My have got all of ³ they / their CDs. '⁴ Us / Our name is Elastic' is the best. ⁵ It / Its cover has got a crocodile on it. The singer is Mary-Lou. ⁶ She / Her is very good. ⁷ She / Her brother Dan is the guitarist. ⁸ He / His has got a lot of guitars. ⁹ He / His favourite guitar is a 1960's Gibson. ¹⁰ It's / Its beautiful. Elastic have two drummers. ¹¹ They / Their names are Nigel and Lucy and ¹² they / their are twins. ¹³ I / My brother Ben loves Elastic too. ¹⁴ We / Our have got tickets* for ¹⁵ they / their show on Tuesday. The tickets are a present from ¹⁶ we / our dad. ¹⁷ I / My dad is the best.

*****ticket** — Eintrittskarte

2 Complete the sentences with the words in the box.

our
your
their
~~my~~
his
its
her

Hello, I'm Polly and this is ...*my*... pet Flopsy.

This is Dana and .... pet Raffles. Isn't he nice?

This is Paul and .... pet Fluffy. Lovely!

This is Sara and Lucy and .... pet rabbit. Isn't he nice?

And what's .... pet?

It's a lizard.

Oh and what does it eat?

.... favourite food are small animals. Cats, dogs, hamsters …

3 Complete the sentences with the possessives.

1 Lillian Britney Spears is ...*my*... favourite singer.

Janice For me too. .... new CD is great.

2 Jim Why is Dan nervous?

Jane .... driving test is today.

3 Henry Who's that over there? I can't see.

Olivia Paul and Liam and .... little sister, I think.

4 Jeff The new zoo is great.

Tina Yes and .... baby elephant is so nice.

 And now go to the CD-ROM and do the *Cartoon for Fun!*

can – can't

Hello! See me on the CD–ROM to discover more about *can – can't* and to learn better when to use them.

Wenn du ausdrücken möchtest, dass jemand etwas kann oder nicht kann verwendest du **can** / **can't**.

+	–
I/You/She/We/They **can** play the piano.	I/You/She/We/They **can't** speak French. (can't = can not)

?	+	–
Can I/You/She/We/They play tennis?	Yes, I/You/She/We/They **can**.	No. I/You/She/We/They **can't**.

1 Look at the picture and write the names of the children.

1 Jack can't sing.
2 Claire can stand on her head.
3 Paul can't juggle.
4 Sue can play the piano.

5 Liam can juggle.
6 Kylie can't stand on her head.
7 Janice can't play the piano.
8 Oliver can sing.

2 **Complete the sentences with the words in the box.**

I can't eat ice cream.

I can't play my computer game.

I can't walk.

I can't speak.

~~I can't climb the tree.~~

I can't eat pizza.

I can't climb the tree. I'm scared.

.... I'm cold.

.... I'm busy.

.... I'm tired.

.... I feel sick.

.... I'm bored.

3 **Put the words in order to make questions.**

1 you / swim / can
<u>Can you swim?</u>
....

2 speak / you / can / French
....

3 English / your / speak / father / can
....

4 horse / you / can / a / ride
....

5 you / can / on / your / hands / walk
....

6 guitar / play / you / the / can
....

7 head / can / your / stand / on / you
....

8 ten / can / cities / the / of / you / English / say / names
....

4 **Write your answers to the questions in** **3** .

And now go to the CD-ROM and do the *Cartoon for Fun!*

21

Present simple

Hello! See me on the CD-ROM to discover more about *present simple* and to learn better when to use it.

Das *Present simple* verwendest du, wenn du über Gewohnheiten, Vorlieben und wiederholte Handlungen sprichst.

Singular	Plural
I **love** London.	We **love** London.
You **eat** fish.	You **eat** fish.

Careful!		
He **loves** Paris.	She **plays** football.	The dog **eats** fish.

1 Find 15 verbs (↑ ↓ ← →). Write them.

R	W	A	I	T	E	S	N	T	A	E	S
A	A	R	R	I	V	B	U	Y	R	F	H
N	T	I	S	I	R	E	R	A	R	W	U
S	C	L	I	M	E	R	T	H	I	F	O
E	H	E	A	B	R	E	K	O	V	A	P
R	B	K	A	E	R	B	U	T	E	L	E
G	R	H	E	A	R	S	N	Y	A	L	P
O	A	W	A	T	C	M	I	O	P	L	R
T	L	A	C	L	I	M	B	L	O	E	I
H	E	Q	U	I	E	R	S	A	B	E	D
A	D	E	G	V	O	S	W	I	T	C	H
H	E	L	P	E	A	B	N	M	O	P	E

1   *watch*   9   ....

2   10   ....

3   11   ....

4   12   ....

5   13   ....

6   14   ....

7   15   ....

8   ....

2 Underline the correct options.

1 We *watch* / *watches* TV in the evening.
2 My father *like* / *likes* music.
3 I *love* / *loves* computer games.
4 You *buy* / *buys* a lot of CDs.

5 Pauline *go* / *goes* to a good school.
6 Alex *climb* / *climbs* trees.
7 They *go* / *goes* to the cinema on Fridays.
8 My dog *play* / *plays* football!

3 Complete with the *He / She / It* forms.

I / You / We / They	play	He / She / It	*plays*
I / You / We / They	arrive	He / She / It	....
I / You / We / They	climb	He / She / It	....
I / You / We / They	leave	He / She / It	....
I / You / We / They	fall	He / She / It	....
I / You / We / They	go	He / She / It	....
I / You / We / They	carry	Hello / She / It	....
I / You / We / They	watch	He / She / It	....

4 **Complete the text with the verbs in the box.**

arrives
climbs
go
goes
~~leaves~~
picks
run
runs
sit
sits
wait
watches
see
hits

Lady Grey's cat, Pepper, [1] ....*leaves*.... the house. It [2] .... to the park. It [3] ....
the birds* in the park. Then, two dogs [4] .... Pepper. Pepper [5] .... away and
[6] .... a tree. Pepper [7] .... in the tree. The dogs [8] .... under the tree.
They [9] .... for Pepper.
Lady Grey [10] .... She [11] .... the dogs on the nose with her umbrella. The dogs
[12] .... away. Lady Grey [13] .... Pepper up. They [14] .... home.

bird — Vogel

5 **Write the verbs in the correct form.**

1 I .... tennis on Sundays. (play)

2 And my sister .... football. (play)

3 I .... the dog at the weekend. (wash)

4 And the dog .... the cat! (wash)

5 I .... Jane's school bag to school. (carry)

6 And my little brother .... my bag! (carry)

7 My father .... to work at 8 o'clock. (go)

8 And my brother and sister .... to school! (go)

23

6 Put the pictures in the correct order to tell a story.

7 Complete the text with the missing letters. Use the pictures in **6** to help you.

Every Monday, Lady Grey ¹ g o e s shopping. Today is Monday – so, Lady Grey ² l _ _ _ _ _ the house and ³ w _ _ _ _ into town. Pepper is in his basket – Pepper ⁴ l _ _ _ _ going shopping! They ⁵ g _ to the supermarket. Lady Grey ⁶ b _ _ _ a lot of things.

Lady Grey ⁷ l _ _ _ _ _ the supermarket. She ⁸ s _ _ _ _ . It's raining! Lady Grey ⁹ l _ _ _ _ in the basket for her umbrella – but it isn't there. It's in the house.

Pepper ¹⁰ j _ _ _ _ out of the basket and ¹¹ r _ _ _ to the house. Lady Grey ¹² w _ _ _ _ outside the supermarket. Pepper ¹³ g _ _ _ into the house. He ¹⁴ p _ _ _ _ up the umbrella and ¹⁵ c _ _ _ _ _ _ _ it to the supermarket.

Lady Grey is very happy. And Pepper is happy too – Lady Grey gives him fish for dinner, his favourite food!

8 Put the verbs in their correct form.

My friend the bird-watcher*

My friend Peter's got an interesting hobby. He ¹ _watches_ (watch) birds.
On Sunday morning, he ² .... (get up) very early. He ³ .... (eat) his breakfast, then he ⁴ .... (take) his binoculars* and ⁵ .... (leave) the house.
He ⁶ .... (walk) in the park or he ⁷ .... (go) into the woods. He ⁸ .... (climb) into a tree and he ⁹ .... (sit) there. He ¹⁰ .... (look) around with his binoculars. Sometimes he ¹¹ .... (wait) for hours and hours!
When a special bird ¹² .... (arrive), Peter's very happy. He ¹³ .... (write) the name of the bird in his book. Then he ¹⁴ .... (go) home for lunch.
Peter really ¹⁵ .... (like) his hobby. What do you think about it?

*bird-watcher – Vogelbeobachter/in   *binoculars – Fernglas

And now go to the CD-ROM and do the **Cartoon for Fun!**

24

Possessive 's

Das **'s** nach einem Namen oder einer Personenbezeichnung verwendest du, um auszudrücken, wem oder zu wem etwas gehört.

It's **John's** dog.

It's **my brother's** computer.

1 Underline the correct options.

1 *My brother's / My brother* favourite computer game is 'Queen's Treasure'.
2 *My mother's / My mother* likes pizza.
3 *My father's / My father* car is blue.
4 *My sister's / My sister* is a good tennis player.
5 *The teacher's / The teacher* favourite word is 'Good'!
6 *Sally's / Sally* dog is black and white.
7 *Sally's / Sally* plays with the dog every day.
8 *Paul's / Paul* favourite sport is volleyball.

2 Complete the sentences. Use the pictures.

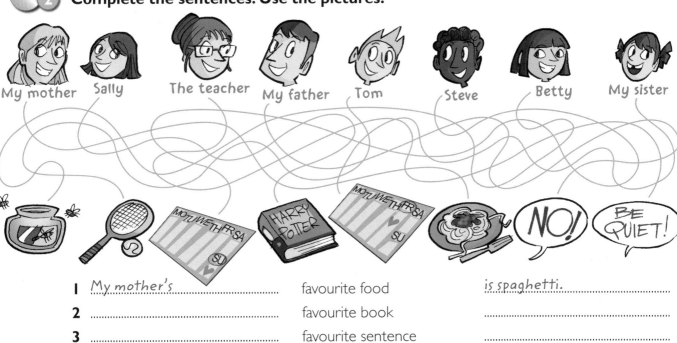

1 My mother's .... favourite food   is spaghetti. ....
2 .... favourite book   ....
3 .... favourite sentence   ....
4 .... favourite word   ....
5 .... favourite sport   ....
6 .... favourite day of the week   ....
7 .... favourite food   ....
8 .... favourite day of the week   ....

And now go to the CD-ROM and do the *Cartoon for Fun!*

Articles *a – an*

Hello! See me on the CD-ROM to discover more about *articles a – an* and to learn better when to use them.

Der unbestimmte Artikel (im Deutschen ein/eine) wird im Englischen durch **a** oder **an** ausgedrückt. Vor Wörtern, die mit einem Vokal (a, e, i, o, u) beginnen, verwendest du **an**. Vor allen anderen verwendest du **a**.

| I've **a n**ew laptop. |
| I've got **an** old laptop. |

1 **Underline the correct word.**

Shopping list
1   <u>a</u> / an   fishing rod
2   a / an   ball
3   a / an   banana
4   a / an   orange pencil
5   a / an   pink pen
6   a / an   newspaper
7   a / an   umbrella
8   a / an   gnome
9   a / an   ice cream

2 **Look at the picture and write what you can see.**

......old shoe......   ....

In the fridge I can see   an ....   and   a ....

....

3 **Complete the text with *a* or *an*.**

There's ¹....*a*.... zoo in our town. It's great. It's got lots of animals. There's ².......... hippo and ³.......... crocodile, ⁴.......... monkey and ⁵.......... old gorilla. There's ⁶.......... elephant. It's really big. There's ⁷.......... orange snake from Africa. It's ⁸.......... beautiful snake. There's ⁹.......... camel and ¹⁰.......... lion and there's ¹¹.......... bear too. But it's not only animals, there are birds too. There's ¹².......... owl and ¹³.......... pelican. There's ¹⁴.......... insect house too. It's got spiders and bugs in it. It's ¹⁵.......... amazing zoo. I love it.

CD-ROM   **And now go to the CD-ROM and do the** *Cartoon for Fun!*

Present simple negative

Hello! See me on the CD–ROM to discover more about *present simple negative* and to learn better when to use it.

So kannst du ausdrücken, dass etwas nicht so ist, oder dass jemand etwas nicht tut oder nicht fühlt. Dafür verwendest du das Hilfsverb **do** mit **not** zusammen mit dem Verb. Du nimmst normalerweise dann auch die Kurzform.

I/You/We/They **don't** speak Italian. (don't = do not)

He/She/It **doesn't** like carrots. (doesn't = does not)

1 Match the pictures and the sentences.

1 He doesn't like carrots.
2 They don't live in a house.
3 It doesn't live in a house.

4 They like carrots.
5 They live in a house.
6 They don't like carrots.

7 She lives in a house.
8 He likes carrots.

2 Make the sentences negative.

1 Jack plays guitar in my band.
Jack doesn't play guitar in my band.

2 My brothers speak French.
....

3 I love Aaron.
....

4 Sally eats lots of vegetables.
....

5 We play tennis every day.
....

6 My dog likes cats.
....

7 They walk to school.
....

8 Dad reads the newspaper in the mornings.
....

27

3 **Complete the sentences with the negative form of the verb and a word from the box.**

German
volleyball
newspapers
horses
~~spinach~~
mornings
drums
red

1 I eat broccoli but I .... *don't eat spinach* .

2 Paul plays guitar but he ....

3 Susie plays tennis but she ....

4 You like nights but you ....

5 My parents speak French but they ....

6 We like pink but we ....

7 I read books but I ....

8 My brothers ride bikes but they ....

4 **Do the animal quiz. Complete with the verbs.**

It ¹ ...*doesn't like*... dogs. (like)

It ² ...*likes*... jumping. (like)

It ³ .... bananas. (eat)

It ⁴ .... grass. (eat)

It ⁵ .... in Australia. (live)

It ⁶ .... in Africa. (live)

It ⁷ .... mangos. (eat)

It ⁸ .... fish. (eat)

It ⁹ .... at the South Pole. (live)

It ¹⁰ .... at the North Pole. (live)

It ¹¹ .... sharks. (like)

It ¹² .... swimming. (like)

5 **Read the text and complete it with the correct form of the verb.**

Saturdays

Ken and Kelly are twins. They're 14. They ¹ ...*live*... (live) in a big house with their mum. Their dad ² ...*doesn't live*... (not live) with them. Ken ³ .... (love) football. He ⁴ .... (play) it every Saturday morning and ⁵ .... (watch) it on TV every Saturday afternoon. Kelly ⁶ .... (not like) football. She ⁷ .... (love) ballet. She ⁸ .... (go) to classes every Saturday morning. In the afternoon she ⁹ .... (not watch) TV with Ken – of course. She ¹⁰ .... (meet) her friends and they ¹¹ .... (go) shopping. They ¹² .... (not buy) – they just ¹³ .... (look) in the shop windows.

And their mum? On Saturday mornings she ¹⁴ .... (drive) Ken to football and then ¹⁵ .... (take) Kelly to ballet. In the afternoon she ¹⁶ .... (cook) dinner and ¹⁷ .... (clean) the house. The children ¹⁸ .... (not help). They're too busy! – That's what they say!

In the evening they all ¹⁹ .... (sit) on the sofa and they ²⁰ .... (watch) a film. Mum ²¹ .... (not see) the end of the film because she ²² .... (fall) asleep. Ken and Kelly ²³ .... (not know) why.

And now go to the CD-ROM and do the *Cartoon for Fun!*

Adverbs of frequency
(always, often, usually, sometimes, never)

Mit Hilfe dieser Wörter kannst du sagen, wie oft jemand etwas macht oder wie oft etwas geschieht.
Achtung: Die Wortstellung im Englischen ist anders als im Deutschen.

0%	→	→	→	100%
never	sometimes	often	usually	always

We **sometimes** go to the cinema on Fridays.

She's **always** happy.

1 Look at the key and the table and then decide if the sentences are **T** (*True*) or **F** (*False*).

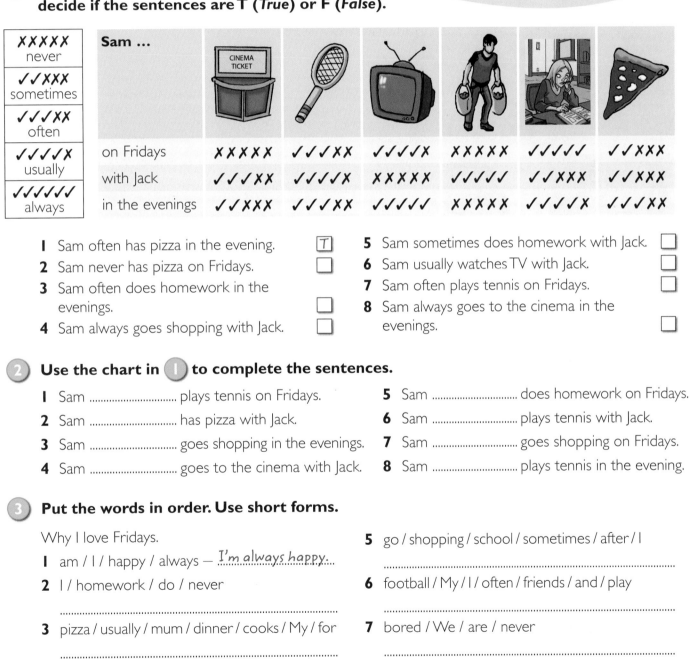

XXXXX never	**Sam ...**						
✓✓XXX sometimes							
✓✓✓XX often							
✓✓✓✓X usually	on Fridays	XXXXX	✓✓✓XX	✓✓✓✓X	XXXXX	✓✓✓✓✓	✓✓XXX
✓✓✓✓✓ always	with Jack	✓✓✓XX	✓✓✓✓X	XXXXX	✓✓✓✓✓	✓✓XXX	✓✓XXX
	in the evenings	✓✓XXX	✓✓✓XX	✓✓✓✓✓	XXXXX	✓✓✓✓X	✓✓✓XX

1 Sam often has pizza in the evening. ☐ T

2 Sam never has pizza on Fridays. ☐

3 Sam often does homework in the evenings. ☐

4 Sam always goes shopping with Jack. ☐

5 Sam sometimes does homework with Jack. ☐

6 Sam usually watches TV with Jack. ☐

7 Sam often plays tennis on Fridays. ☐

8 Sam always goes to the cinema in the evenings. ☐

2 Use the chart in ① to complete the sentences.

1 Sam .... plays tennis on Fridays.

2 Sam .... has pizza with Jack.

3 Sam .... goes shopping in the evenings.

4 Sam .... goes to the cinema with Jack.

5 Sam .... does homework on Fridays.

6 Sam .... plays tennis with Jack.

7 Sam .... goes shopping on Fridays.

8 Sam .... plays tennis in the evening.

3 Put the words in order. Use short forms.

Why I love Fridays.

1 am / I / happy / always — *I'm always happy.*

2 I / homework / do / never

....

3 pizza / usually / mum / dinner / cooks / My / for

....

4 too / We / have / ice cream / sometimes

....

5 go / shopping / school / sometimes / after / I

....

6 football / My / I / often / friends / and / play

....

7 bored / We / are / never

....

8 We / are / weekend / about / excited / always / the

....

4 Read the sentences. Correct the ones with mistakes.

A week in the life of Rebecca Rich

1 On Mondays, often she goes shopping. ✗
   On Mondays, she often goes shopping.

2 On Tuesdays, she often washes her dogs. ✓

3 On Wednesdays, she always is hot.

4 On Thursdays, she sees usually her friends.

5 On Fridays, she sometimes plays sport.

6 On Saturday nights, she is never at home.

7 On Sundays, she eats often in the best restaurant.

8 She always is bored.

5 Rewrite the sentences. Put in the adverb of frequency.

1 I'm late to school. (never)
   I'm never late to school.

2 Dad watches TV in the evenings. (often)

3 The children are tired after school. (sometimes)

4 We wash the car Sunday. (always)

5 She's bored at the weekend. (usually)

6 My sister eats carrots. (never)

7 I do my homework before dinner. (usually)

8 It's cold in December. (always)

6 Complete the sentences with an adverb of frequency to make them true for you.

1 I'm .... bored in the school holidays.

2 I .... shout at my friends.

3 I .... spend a lot of time on my homework.

4 I'm .... hungry when I get up.

5 I .... watch TV after school.

6 I .... eat junk food at the weekend.

7 I'm .... happy on a Monday.

8 I .... read a newspaper in the morning.

And now go to the CD-ROM and do the Cartoon for Fun!

Present simple questions & short answers

Fragen, die mit ja oder nein zu beantworten sind, werden mit **do** oder **does** gebildet (Ausnahme: Fragen mit **to be**). Fragen zu **he/she/it** (3. Person Singular) bildest du mit **does**, alle anderen Fragen mit **do**.

Du verwendest meist Kurzantworten mit **Yes** oder **No**, um auf diese Fragen zu reagieren (du brauchst in der Antwort also nicht den ganzen Satz zu wiederholen).

> **Hello! See me on the CD-ROM to discover more about *present simple questions – short answers* and to learn better when to use them.**

?	+	–
Do you go to my school?	Yes, I **do**.	No, I **don't**.
Does he/she/it like ice cream?	Yes, he/she/it **does**.	No, he/she/it **doesn't**.
Do I/we live near you?	Yes, you **do**.	No, you **don't**.
Do they play tennis every day?	Yes, they **do**.	No, they **don't**.

1 Underline the correct words.

1 *Do / Does* he live in London?
2 *Do / Does* they like peas?
3 *Do / Does* your mum speak German?
4 *Do / Does* Nigel and Tim want to go to the cinema?
5 *Do / Does* the shop open at 10 a.m.?
6 *Do / Does* your parents like rock music?
7 *Do / Does* the film finish before 10 p.m.?
8 *Do / Does* you like blue?

2 Match the questions and the answers.

1 Do they speak Spanish?
2 Do you know Mary?
3 Does she like Jim?
4 Does your school start at 9 a.m.?
5 Does Paul want a sandwich?
6 Do we have English today?
7 Do I know Robin?
8 Does your mum cook pasta well?

a No, it doesn't.
b No, he doesn't. He isn't hungry.
c No, we don't. We have it on Fridays.
d Yes, you do. He's Henry's brother.
e No, they don't. They speak Portuguese.
f Yes, she does. She's Italian!
g Yes, I do. She's my sister's best friend.
h Yes, she does. They're good friends.

3 Write the answers.

1 Do you like broccoli? (✗)
   No, I don't.

2 Does Anne go to your school? (✓)
   ....

3 Does Tim play football well? (✓)
   ....

4 Do they buy their own clothes? (✗)
   ....

5 Do you know Evan? (✓)
   ....

6 Does your mum take you to school? (✗)
   ....

7 Do Jane and Fred like the Beatles? (✓)
   ....

8 Does Lillian eat meat? (✗)
   ....

4 Complete the dialogue with *do*, *does*, *don't* or *doesn't*.

Interviewer ¹..........*Do*........ you buy your own clothes?
Daisy No, I ²..................... .
Interviewer ³..................... your mum buy your clothes?
Daisy Yes, she ⁴..................... . And my dad buys me clothes sometimes too.
Interviewer Really? ⁵..................... you like the clothes your dad buys for you?
Daisy Yes, I ⁶..................... . He always buys me nice clothes.
Interviewer ⁷..................... he buy you dresses and pink T-shirts, clothes like that?

Daisy No he ⁸.....................! He buys me cool jeans and black T-shirts.
Interviewer What about your mum? ⁹..................... she buy you cool clothes too?
Daisy No, she ¹⁰..................... . She buys me dresses and pink T-shirts.
Interviewer What's wrong with pink?
Daisy Everything. I hate pink!

5 Look at the pictures and write questions and the answers.

1 Ricky Starr / drive a nice car
Q *Does Ricky Starr drive a nice car?*   A *Yes, he does.*

2 Ricky Starr / wear a silly hat?
Q .... A ....

3 Ricky Starr / wear shoes?
Q .... A ....

4 Ricky Starr / speak French
Q .... A ....

5 They / want Ricky Starr's autograph*
Q .... A ....

6 They / like Ricky Starr
Q .... A ....

7 They / like Ricky Starr
Q .... A ....

8 Ricky Starr / happy?
Q .... A ....

> *autograph* – Autogramm

6 Put the words in order to make questions.

1 opera / do / like / you
Do you like opera?

2 meat / eat / you / do
....

3 clothes / do / wear / you / red
....

4 tennis / do / play / you
....

5 cook / does / your / father
....

6 English / your / friend / does / speak / best
....

7 friends / your / same / all / school / go / to / do / the
....

8 headmaster / name / know / does / your / your
....

7 Write your answers to the questions in **6**.

And now go to the CD-ROM and do the *Cartoon for Fun!*

Question words (*What / Where / How often*)

Wenn du eine Frage stellst, auf die du eine ausführlichere Antwort erwartest als nur ja oder nein, verwendest du die Fragewörter **What ...? Where ...? How ...?**.

What does your dog eat?

Where does your dog sleep?

How often does your dog have a bath?

1 **Write the words in the correct order.**

1 your / what / name / is
What is your name ?

2 do / live / where / you
.... ?

3 often / do / how / come here / you
.... ?

4 eat / hamsters / what / do
.... ?

5 go / you / how / do / to the cinema / often
.... ?

6 pet snake / you / do / keep / your / where
.... ?

2 **Complete the questions.**

A ¹....... How .... are you?

B I'm fine, thanks.

A ²...................... is your name?

B Alison.

A ³...................... do you live?

B In Birmingham.

A ⁴...................... pets have you got?

B A hamster and two white mice.

A ⁵...................... do they live?

B In a cage in my room.

A ⁶...................... do you feed them?

B Every day.

A ⁷...................... do they eat?

B Special pet food.

A ⁸...................... do they leave the cage?

B Three times a week — but don't tell my mum!

3 **Write your answers to the questions.**

1 What pets have you got?
I've got ....

2 Where do you live?
....

3 What clothes do you wear to school?
....

4 Where does your best friend live?
....

5 How often do you eat fish?
....

6 How often do you go to the cinema?
....

And now go to the CD-ROM and do the *Cartoon for Fun!*

33

Object pronouns

Personalpronomen sind Stellvertreter von Personen, aber auch von Tieren oder Dingen. Sie haben zwei Formen, je nachdem wie sie in einem Satz gebraucht werden.

Subject	Object
I	**me**
you	**you**
he	**him**
she	**her**

Subject	Object
it	**it**
we	**us**
you	**you**
they	**them**

1 **Underline the correct options.**

1 We haven't got cats at home — we don't like *it* / *them* / *they*.

2 I've got a mouse — I keep *it* / *them* / *me* in a cage.

3 Mr Brown's a good teacher — we really like *us* / *him* / *her*.

4 It's late now. Can I phone *you* / *me* / *it* tomorrow?

5 This is my new computer — do you like *him* / *her* / *it*?

6 My mother's in the garden — let's go and ask *she* / *him* / *her*.

7 We're going to the cinema. Come with *you* / *him* / *us*.

8 Look at those dogs! I'm scared of *them* / *it* / *you*.

2 **Replace the underlined words with the correct object pronouns.**

My animal friends

My name's Patsy and I love animals!

I've got a cat called Snowy – she's all white. I love Snowy and she loves ~~Patsy~~ [1] ....*me*........ too. I feed ~~Snowy~~ [2] .... three times a day.

I've got some fish too – I feed ~~the fish~~ [3] .... once a day. They live in a fish tank – the tank gets dirty and I have to clean ~~the tank~~ [4] .... once a week.

My brother's got a snake in his room – it's called Spike. My brother feeds ~~Spike~~ [5] .... twice a week, but I don't know what Spike eats. My brother doesn't tell ~~Patsy~~ [6] .... , and I don't ask ~~my brother~~ [7] .... !

Mr Potts is an old man who lives in the same street. He's got two big black dogs. My brother and I take the dogs for walks and on Sundays we wash ~~the dogs~~ [8] .... Mr Potts pays ~~my brother and me~~ [9] .... £10 a week.

And now go to the CD-ROM and do the *Cartoon for Fun!*

34

this, that / these, those

Hello! See me on the CD-ROM to discover more about *this, that / these, those* and to learn better when to use them.

This und **these** verwendest du, wenn du über etwas sprichst, das nahe ist.
That und **those** verwendest du, wenn du über etwas spricht, das weiter weg ist.

I like **this** jumper here.	I like **that** jumper over there.
I like **these** shoes here.	I like **those** shoes over there.

1 **Write the sentences into the speech bubbles.**

I think this apple is a bit old.
OK, can we try those shoes, over there?
I want that fish over there.
OK, try one of those apples.

Would you like this lollipop?
~~Do you like these goldfish?~~
No, I'd like that lollipop over there.
I think these shoes are too big.

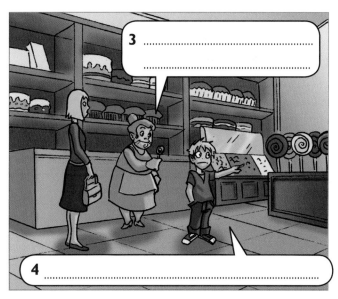

2 Underline the correct word.

1 I want *those* / *that* trainers with the blue strip.
2 Does *those* / *that* dog bite?
3 Can I have *this* / *these* apple?
4 *That* / *These* is my favourite CD.

5 Do you want *that* / *these* shoes?
6 Are *that* / *those* carrots good?
7 I don't like *this* / *these* insects.
8 I know *that* / *these* boy.

3 Complete with *this*, *that*, *these* or *those*.

1 Are you sure ....*this*........ car is brand new?

2 I think .... hamster is too big for its cage.

3 Do you like .... paintings I did for you?

4 I don't think .... girls are very happy with me.

5 Does .... hat look good on me?

6 Be careful with .... eggs. You don't want to drop them.

7 Now, ... ice cream looks good!

8 .... trousers aren't very comfortable.

And now go to the CD-ROM and do the *Cartoon for Fun!*

How much is/are ...?

Eine Frage mit **How much ...?** verwendest du, wenn du wissen möchtest was etwas kostet.
Du musst darauf achten, ob es sich um einen oder mehrere Gegenstände handelt.

How much **are** these/those jeans?   How much **is** this/that T-shirt?

1 Underline the correct word.

1 How much *is* / *are* the puppies?   **5** How much *is* / *are* the umbrellas?

2 How much *is* / *are* the orange?   **6** How much *is* / *are* the newspaper?

3 How much *is* / *are* the guitar?   **7** How much *is* / *are* the fishing rods?

4 How much *is* / *are* the scissors?   **8** How much *is* / *are* the pen?

2 Read the dialogue and complete with *is* or *are*.

Assistant Hello, what would you like to eat?

Claire How much ¹...*are*.. the cheese sandwiches?

Assistant They're £3.50.

Claire And how much ².......... the cheese and tomato sandwiches?

Assistant They're £3.50 too.

Claire How much ³.......... a ham sandwich?

Assistant A ham sandwich ⁴.......... £3.50. All the sandwiches ⁵.......... £3.50.

Claire What about the pizza? How much ⁶.......... a cheese pizza?

Assistant A cheese pizza ⁷.......... £3.50.

Claire How much ⁸.......... the ham pizzas?

Assistant They're £3.50 too. All the pizzas ⁹.......... £3.50.

Claire OK. So how much ¹⁰.......... the chicken soup?

Assistant The chicken soup ¹¹.......... £3.50.

Claire And how much ¹².......... the tomato soup?

Assistant £3.50. All the soups ¹³.......... £3.50. Everything in the shop ¹⁴.......... £3.50. Look at the sign.

Claire Oh.

Assistant So what can I get you to eat?

Claire Nothing. I'm not hungry any more.

3 Follow the lines to find out the prices. Then write questions and answers.

£1.00   £1.50   £2.00   £1.90   £1.20   £1.00

£4.00   £2.40

Q <u>How much are the scissors?</u>

A <u>They're £1.90.</u>

Q How much ....

A It's ....

Q ....

A ....

And now go to the CD-ROM and do the *Cartoon for Fun!*

37

Present continuous

Hello! See me on the CD-ROM to discover more about the *present continuous* and to learn better when to use it.

Wenn du beschreiben möchtest, was jemand gerade tut oder was gerade in diesem Augenblick passiert, musst du im Englischen die sogenannte *continuous* Form des Verbs verwenden. Diese setzt sich zusammen aus **am/are/is** und der **–ing** Form des Verbs.

+	–
I**'m playing** football. (= I am)	I**'m not playing** tennis. (= I **am not**)
You**'re**/We**'re**/They**'re watching** TV. (= We **are**)	You**'re**/We**'re**/They **aren't watching** a DVD. (= We **are not**)
He**'s**/She**'s cooking** dinner. (= He/She **is**)	He/She **isn't** listening to music. (= He/She **is not**)

Fragen und Kurzantworten werden gebildet wie beim Verb **be**.

?	Short answers
Are you **cooking** dinner?	**Yes**, I **am**. / No, I**'m not**.
Is Tony/Sandra **reading** a book?	**Yes**, he/she **is**. / No, he/she **isn't**.
Are Nick and James **playing** tennis?	**Yes**, they **are**. / No, they **aren't**.

❶ Write the sentences under the pictures.

Gillie is calling her dad.
Gillie is watching a DVD.
There's mum — she's looking for her key!

Someone is knocking on the window.
Gillie is walking to the window.
Dad is having a shower.

2 Complete the sentences with words and phrases from the box.

he doing
karate
doing a sport
He's trying
playing football
gymnastics
a picture in a book
a karate suit
are dancing

Look at Tony's family. Today they're all doing sports. Becky and mum are doing
1... . Dad's wearing 2... .
He's looking at 3... and he's learning
4... . Jake is outside in the garden. He's
5... . Fluffy and Spotty, the two cats,
6... . Look at Floyd, the snake. What's
7... ? No, he isn't 8.. .
9... to get some chocolate.

3 Circle the correct answer.

1 They *isn't* / *aren't* having a gymnastics lesson at the moment.
2 I'm *not* / *aren't* doing my homework right now.
3 Are you *enjoying* / *enjoy** the party?
4 The cats *aren't* / *isn't* sleeping* on the bed.
5 *Is* / *Are* Gemma watching TV?
6 We *isn't* / *aren't* playing basketball today.
7 *Is* / *Are* you making a sandwich?
8 Alice isn't *talking* / *talk* to Diana at the moment.

> ***enjoy** — Spaß haben an
> ***sleep** — schlafen

4 Make the sentences negative.

1 We're watching TV.
We aren't watching TV.

2 They're swimming.
....

3 I'm keeping fit at the moment.
....

4 Susan is learning karate.
....

5 Jane and Tim are trying to do gymnastics.
....

6 John's playing tennis with his friend.
....

7 I'm listening to my CDs.
....

8 They're singing a song.

5 **Complete the questions and the short answers with the correct form of be.**

1 A .... you having your lunch now?

B Yes, I .... Phone me again tonight.

2 A .... your mum cooking?

B No, she .... Dad's making lunch today.

3 A .... your brother learning to drive?

B No, he .... He's only 16.

4 A .... you waiting for me?

B No, I .... I'm waiting for Alan.

5 A .... James winning the race?

B Yes, he .... He's a really good runner.

6 A .... your parents watching TV?

B No, they .... So we can watch a DVD now, OK?

7 A .... I sitting in your place?

B Yes, you .... But it's OK!

8 A .... you and your sister learning to ski?

B Yes, we .... And we're getting better!

6 **Complete the sentences with am, is or are. Use short forms where possible.**

> I am writing = I**'m** writing
> You are writing = you**'re** writing
> He is writing = he**'s** writing

Hi James,

We're in London for the weekend. I'..*m*.. in my room. Joanne and Claire are with mum. They ¹........ shopping in Oxford Street. Dad ²........ not shopping. He ³........ watching a football match on TV. And what ⁴........ I doing? Guess! Yes, I ⁵........ writing emails. And I ⁶........ surfing the Internet. Wait a moment. Now I ⁷........ looking out of the window. There are lots of people. They ⁸........ all wearing very warm clothes. It ⁹........ cold here, and it ¹⁰........ raining. What's that? Now I can see a double-decker bus. Some people ¹¹........ doing a sightseeing tour. But they ¹²........ getting wet! Poor guys!

They're enjoying* their sightseeing tour!

> ***enjoy** — Spaß haben an

7 **Complete the answers.**

1 A Where's John?

B ..*He's playing*.............. football with his friends. (play)

2 A Where are Tony and Nick?

B .... to music. (listen)

3 A What's Thomas doing?

B .... TV. (watch)

4 A Let's go to the cinema.

B Sorry, I can't. .... my homework. (do)

5 A Can we talk now?

B Sure. .... anything important. (not do)

6 A Is Polly in the park?

B Yes. .... her bicycle. (ride)

7 A Let's go for a walk.

B Good idea. .... (not rain)

8 A Why doesn't Paula answer the teacher?

B Because .... ! (not listen)

8 Circle the correct answer.

1 Mum! The telephone *rings* / *'s ringing*! Can you answer it? I *watch* / *'m watching* television.

2 Mary *writes* / *'s writing* emails every day. Today she *writes* / *'s writing* to her friend Samantha.

3 Paul *goes* / *'s going* to see his grandparents today. He *travels* / *'s travelling* by train.

4 My mum and I *go* / *are going* shopping every Saturday. Usually we *buy* / *'re buying* clothes or books.

5 I *go* / *'m going* to the cinema once a week. My brother usually *goes* / *'s going* with me.

6 My sister *reads* / *'s reading* three books every week. At the moment, she *reads* / *'s reading* a book about horses.

7 This is a great party. All my friends *dance* / *are dancing* and we *have* / *'re having* a good time.

8 Gail and Sarah *play* / *are playing* football at the moment. But Andrea *doesn't like* / *isn't liking* football so she *doesn't play* / *isn't playing* with them.

9 Circle the correct answer.

Hi Jeremy,

Well, here we are on holiday. We're in France – well, we're on an island near France. It's called Ile de Re. We ¹*come* / *'re coming* here every year – remember? We always ²*stay* / *'re staying* at the same campsite, it's called 'The Blue Dreams' campsite. It's OK – but you know I ³*don't enjoy* / *'m not enjoying* camping very much!

Well, today it ⁴*rains* / *'s raining* so I ⁵*sit* / *'m sitting* in our tent and I ⁶*write* / *'m writing* to you. Mum and dad aren't here, they're in the town, they ⁷*do* / *'re doing* some shopping. They ⁸*buy* / *'re buying* food for dinner tonight – spaghetti, for sure (we ⁹*have* / *'re having* spaghetti for dinner every night when we're on holiday – boring!!) My brother Eddie? He's in the next tent. He ¹⁰*talks* / *'s talking* to a girl called Anita. She's French – I think she ¹¹*lives* / *'s living* in Toulouse or somewhere. Anyway, Eddie really ¹²*likes* / *'s liking* her. Just a minute – there's a noise! Someone ¹³*shouts* / *'s shouting*. It's Anita – and I don't think she is very happy. And here comes Eddie – and he ¹⁴*laughs* / *'s laughing* about something! OK, time for me to stop. I'll write again tomorrow! Bye!!!!!!

10 Complete the dialogues. Write the verbs in the present simple or present continuous form.

1 **A** Have you got a pet?

  B Yes, a crocodile. It .... in a big pond in my garden. (live)

2 **A** Is Peter doing his homework?

  B No, he isn't. He .... computer games. (play)

3 **A** .... you and Kate .... an instrument? (play)

  B No, we don't. We .... in a band. (sing)

4 **A** Are you reading?

  B No, I'm not. I .... my homework. (do)

5 **A** .... you .... TV? (watch)

  B Yes, I am. It's a great film!

6 **A** Does Sandra wear dresses?

  B No, never. She always .... jeans. (wear)

11 Complete the dialogue. Write the verbs in the present simple or present continuous form.

Paul Hi, Helen. Where ¹ .... *are you going* .... ? (go)

Helen To my karate class. I ² .... (do) karate every Friday afternoon.

Paul Cool! ³ .... you .... (wear) special clothes for karate?

Helen Yes — white trousers and a white shirt.

Paul Yes, of course. I ⁴ .... (know) that! Silly me.

Helen It's OK. ⁵ .... you .... (play) any sports, Paul?

Paul Yes — football, of course. But at the moment I ⁶ .... (learn) to ski, too.

Helen Really? But we live in London — you can't ski here!

Paul No — but my dad ⁷ .... (go) to Switzerland every January. And he says that I can with him next year.

Helen Brilliant!

And now go to the CD-ROM and do the Cartoon for Fun!

42

Ordinal numbers

Ordnungszahlen (der/die/das erste, zweite, dritte usw.) werden im Englischen durch spezielle Endungen gebildet. Merkregel: Hänge beim Schreiben an die Zahl 1 **–st**, an 2 **–nd** und an 3 **–rd** an, sonst immer **–th**!

one ➜ **first**	two ➜ **second**	three ➜ **third**
four ➜ four**th**	five ➜ fi**fth**	seven ➜ seven**th**
ten ➜ ten**th**	eleven ➜ eleven**th**	twelve ➜ twel**fth**
twenty ➜ twent**ieth**	twenty-one ➜ twenty-**first**	thirty-four ➜ thirty-**fourth**

1 **Find ten ordinal numbers (➜ or ↓).**

A	S	E	C	O	N	D	S	T
T	W	E	L	F	T	H	F	W
H	T	E	P	I	E	S	O	E
R	H	C	O	X	I	E	U	N
F	I	R	S	T	T	V	R	T
I	R	G	I	Z	G	E	T	I
F	D	I	X	T	H	N	H	E
T	E	N	T	E	N	T	H	T
H	I	X	H	H	A	H	O	H

2 **Match the numbers and ordinal numbers. Draw lines.**

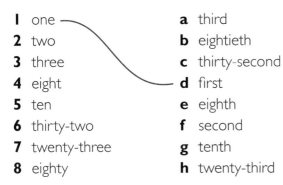

1 one   **a** third
2 two   **b** eightieth
3 three   **c** thirty-second
4 eight   **d** first
5 ten   **e** eighth
6 thirty-two   **f** second
7 twenty-three   **g** tenth
8 eighty   **h** twenty-third

3 **Complete the table.**

6	....	21	....	....	....	70	44
six	two	....	....	....	....	....	....
6th	....	21st	....	5th	....	70th	....
sixth	....	....	seventeenth	....	third	....	....

4 **Complete the sentences.**

1 Monday is the first day of the week, so Tuesday is the ....*second*.......... day.

2 And Friday is the .... day.

3 The first month of the year is ....

4 And September is the .... month.

5 Saturday is the .... day of the week, and Sunday is the .... day.

6 May is the .... month of the year, and August is the .... month.

Time prepositions (*in / on / at*)

Wenn du sagen möchtest, wann etwas stattfindet, verwendest du **at**, **in** oder **on**.

My birthday is **on** February 12ᵗʰ / May 28ᵗʰ / September 5ᵗʰ.

My sister's birthday is **in** December / April / June.

The film starts **at** 7 o'clock / half past eight / six forty-five.

We have Maths **in** the morning / **in** the afternoon.

We go to bed late **at** night.

1 **Underline the correct options.**

1 I usually get up *in / at / on* seven thirty every day.

2 School starts *in / at / on* 8.45.

3 My birthday is *in / at / on* March 17ᵗʰ.

4 We don't go to school *in / at / on* Saturday or Sunday.

5 The film ends *in / at / on* half past ten.

6 In Brazil, there are school holidays *in / at / on* January.

7 My dad's birthday is *in / at / on* February 28ᵗʰ.

8 *In / At / On* Saturdays, I play football *in / at / on* the afternoon.

9 Our national holiday is *in / at / on* September the 7ᵗʰ.

10 You must come home *in / at / on* eleven o'clock.

11 We always go skiing *in / at / on* December.

12 We have dinner *in / at / on* 9 o'clock *in / at / on* night.

2 **Write the correct preposition (*in / at / on*) in each space.**

I've got an amazing family! Well, I think we're amazing, and it's because of our birthdays. My mum's birthday is ¹ ..on.. the 12ᵗʰ of June, and my father's is ² .... the 12ᵗʰ of June too – only, my dad is two years older than my mum.
OK, that's not very special – but wait!
My mother's got a sister – my Aunt Louise – and they're twins*! They were born* ³ .... 12ᵗʰ of June, of course – my mum was born ⁴ .... 3 o'clock ⁵ .... the morning, and my aunt was born ⁶ .... half past three.

I've got four brothers – Jimmy, Timmy, Ed and Ted. Jimmy and Timmy are twins, too – they were born ⁷ .... 17ᵗʰ of September. And guess what? Yes – Jimmy was born ⁸ .... 3 o'clock and Timmy was born ⁹ .... half past three! (But my twin brothers were born ¹⁰ .... the afternoon, not ¹¹ .... the morning!)

Ed and Ted aren't twins – Ed is sixteen, and Ted is only eight. But – Ed and Ted were both* born ¹² .... 11 o'clock ¹³ .... night, and they were both born ¹⁴ .... December 1ˢᵗ! Isn't that amazing?!

> ***twins** – Zwillinge
> ***(was/were) born** – (ist/sind) geboren
> ***both** – beide

And now go to the CD-ROM and do the Cartoon for Fun!

44

Past simple – *was / were*

Hello! See me on the CD-ROM to discover more about *past simple – was / were* and to learn better when to use it.

Wenn du sagen willst, was war (bzw. nicht war) verwendest du die *past simple* Form von **to be**.

+	–	?
I/He/She/It **was** at home last night.	I/He/She/It **wasn't** at home last night.	**Was** I/he/she/it …?
You/We/They **were** very angry.	You/We/They **weren't** very angry.	**Were** you/we/they …?

1 Write the days of the week under the pictures.

1 On Monday I was in Paris.
2 On Tuesday Mike and Henry were in Paris.
3 On Wednesday Paul was in Pisa.

4 On Thursday we were in Pisa.
5 On Friday Julia was in Sydney.
6 On Saturday they were in Sydney.

a ....

b ....

c ....

d ....

e ....

f ....

2 Where were these people yesterday afternoon? Write sentences using the words in the box to help you.

in the garden	in a field
on a pond	at a concert
at the cinema	~~in bed~~
on the farm	at school

1 Ben *was in bed.* ....

2 June and Simon ....

3 Mrs Gladstone ....

4 Kevin and Lucy ....

5 Mr Thomas ....

6 May and Annabel ....

7 Liam and Fred ....

8 Tina ....

3 **Answer the questions about the people in** ②**. Use short answers.**

I Was Ben at the cinema?
No, he wasn't.

5 Was Mr Thomas at the cinema?
....

2 Were June and Simon on a farm?
....

6 Were May and Annabel at a concert?
....

3 Was Mrs Gladstone in bed?
....

7 Were Liam and Fred on a pond?
....

4 Were Kevin and Lucy at school?
....

8 Was Tina in a field?
....

4 **Read the story and underline the correct words.**

It was 9 p.m. and Simon ¹ *was / were* home. He ² *was / were* a bit nervous. The front door to his house ³ *was / were* open and all the lights ⁴ *was / were* on. The kitchen ⁵ *was / were* very messy. There ⁶ *was / were* coats on the floor and there ⁷ *was / were* dirty cups on the table. The door to living room ⁸ *wasn't / weren't* open. Simon ⁹ *wasn't / weren't* nervous now, he ¹⁰ *was / were* scared. He needed to call the police. Where ¹¹ *was / were* his phone? Oh no. It ¹² *wasn't / weren't* in his coat. It ¹³ *was / were* in his bedroom. ¹⁴ *Was / Were* that a noise* from behind the living room door? There ¹⁵ *was / were* another noise. Eeeeeeeeeek. The door ¹⁶ *was / were* now open. The lights ¹⁷ *wasn't / weren't* on in the living room. It ¹⁸ *was / were* dark. He needed to get in the car and drive to the police! Where ¹⁹ *was / were* his car keys? They ²⁰ *wasn't / weren't* in his coat. They ²¹ *was / were* in the bedroom too. Suddenly there ²² *was / were* a big flash*. The lights in the living room ²³ *was / were* on. There ²⁴ *was / were* lots of people. They ²⁵ *was / were* all his friends – 'Surprise'. It ²⁶ *was / were* a party, a surprise party for him. Simon ²⁷ *was / were* confused*. Today ²⁸ *wasn't / weren't* his birthday. His birthday ²⁹ *was / were* tomorrow!

> *noise* – Geräusch **flash** – Blitzlicht **confused** – verwirrt

5 **Make the sentences negative.**

I I was happy yesterday.
I wasn't happy yesterday.

5 We were ill after the meal in that restaurant.
....

2 Nigel was hungry after the walk.
....

6 I was at home yesterday at 6 p.m.
....

3 Mum and dad were at my school this morning.
....

7 It was very hot in Spain for our holidays.
....

4 They were excited about my birthday.
....

8 The party was excellent.
....

6 Complete the dialogue with *was*, *were*, *wasn't* or *weren't*.

Inspector Where [1] ....*were*.... you at 8 p.m. yesterday?

Mr Green I [2] .... at home with my wife.

Inspector At home.

Mr Green Yes, we [3] .... in the living room.

Inspector And [4] .... your children with you?

Mr Green Julia [5] .... She [6] .... at a friend's house.

Inspector And Brian? [7] .... he at home?

Mr Green Yes, Brian [8] .... at home. He [9] .... in his bedroom.

Inspector What about the maid and the cook? Where [10] .... they?

Mr Green I don't know. But they [11] .... in the house.

Inspector How do you know that?

Mr Green Because they don't work here on Saturdays.

Inspector But yesterday [12] .... Sunday.

Mr Green Oh, yes, of course.

Inspector And the cook [13] .... in the kitchen at 8 p.m. She says you [14] .... in the garage at 8 p.m. — in the garage where the body [15] ....

Mr Green It [16] .... my wife. It [17] .... me!

Inspector Interesting. She says it [18] .... you. Please come with me to the police station, Mr Green.

7 Put the words in order to make questions.

1 yesterday / bored / you / Were

Were you bored yesterday?

2 were / Where / you / at / 8 p.m. / yesterday

....?

3 Sunday / you / afternoon / were / Who / with / on

....?

4 morning / you / at / Where / 8 a.m. / were / this

....?

5 friend / your / yesterday / best / Was / happy

....?

6 school / Were / at / afternoon / yesterday / you

....?

8 Answer the questions in ⑦ about you.

Example *No, I wasn't. I was excited. It was my sister's birthday.*

1 ....

2 ....

3 ....

4 ....

5 ....

6 ....

CD-ROM

And now go to the CD-ROM and do the *Cartoon for Fun!*

Past simple – regular verbs

Hello! See me on the CD-ROM to discover more about *past simple – regular verbs* and to learn better when to use them.

Zum Erzählen einer Geschichte verwendest du das *past simple*.
Die *past simple* Form regelmäßiger Verben wird durch Anhängen der Endung **-ed** gebildet.

Present	Past	Present	Past	Present	Past
walk	walk**ed**	play	play**ed**	listen	listen**ed**
arrive	arriv**ed**	change	chang**ed**	stop	stop**ped**
study	stud**ied**	carry	carr**ied**	try	tr**ied**

I Read the story. Put the pictures in order.

A lucky day

**Yesterday morning was great.
Lots of things happened!**

I jumped out of bed at seven o'clock. I looked out of the window – rain, rain, rain! So I played my favourite computer game for half an hour. I wanted to play longer, but mum shouted: 'Amy, your breakfast is ready!' After breakfast, I listened to music (I've got a great new CD) and watched TV for a bit.

Then the weather changed. It was sunny! So I walked to the park. I phoned Paul and waited for him. He arrived ten minutes later with his dog Bonkers. Bonkers chased a squirrel* up a tree – it was very funny!

Then Paul noticed something. There was a cat in the tree too. I climbed the tree, picked up the cat and carried it down to the ground again.

We tried to find the owner of the cat, but no luck. I asked my mum: 'Mum, can I keep the cat?' and she said 'OK'. So now I've got a cat called Lucky at home!

*****squirrel** – Eichhörnchen

48

Underline the correct options in each sentence.

1 I *phone / phoned* my friend Paul every day — yesterday I *phone / phoned* him at six o'clock in the morning!

2 Yesterday I was a bit angry with Jenny. I always *walk / walked* to school with her, but yesterday she *walks / walked* to school with Harry Smith!

3 Sometimes Mark *plays / played* football well. Last Saturday, he *plays / played* really badly!

4 Our dog is great — when we go shopping, he always *carries / carried* the shopping basket. Last weekend, he *carries / carried* a really heavy basket!

5 We usually *study / studied* for an hour every night — but yesterday we *study / studied* for three hours.

6 When my cat was little, she *chases / chased* birds. Now she *chases / chased* dogs!

7 There's an interesting programme on TV. Every week, they *interview / interviewed* a famous person. Last week they *interview / interviewed* my favourite film star.

8 The teacher was surprised yesterday when Johnny *asks / asked* a question. Johnny never *asks / asked* questions in class!

Read the story. Write one of the verbs in each space — but you have to unjumble the letters!

postdep	adesk
tendaw	shepud
outshed	koledo
ghedlau	sdeach
klawde	hondep
~~diedust~~	dietr
pudmej	nephadpe
detrsat	drivear

Last night I ¹......*studied*...... for two hours in my bedroom. I was very tired. I ².......................... to go out – I needed some fresh air. I ³.......................... out of our house and I ⁴.......................... to walk along my street. Suddenly a car ⁵.......................... near me. Two men ⁶.......................... out of the car. They ⁷.......................... at a boy: 'Get in the car!' The boy was frightened and he ⁸.......................... to run away. But the men ⁹.......................... him into the car and the car drove away.

I ¹⁰.......................... the car for 100 metres, but it was too fast. So I ¹¹.......................... the police. When the police ¹².......................... , they ¹³.......................... me lots of questions. The first question was: 'What's your name?' The second question was: 'What ¹⁴.......................... here?' The third question was: 'Sally! Do you want your dinner?' It was a strange question. I ¹⁵.......................... round – my mother was at my bedroom door. 'Sally – you were asleep!' she said. We ¹⁶.......................... a lot. It was just a dream!

Past simple – irregular verbs

Es gibt auch Verben, deren *past simple* Form nicht durch Anhängen der Endung **-ed** gebildet werden. Diese Verben nennt man unregelmäßige Verben. Ihre Formen lernst du am besten auswendig.

I/You/He/She/We/They **told** a great joke. – Not ~~telled~~.

I/You/He/She/We/They **bought** a new coat. – Not ~~buyed~~.

1 **Underline the irregular verb in each sentence.**

1 They <u>went</u> to the park and hired a boat.
2 He sat on the chair and waited.
3 They watched TV and ate a pizza.
4 She walked into the house and put her bag down.
5 I phoned Jane and told her everything.
6 He said he wanted an ice cream.
7 We held hands and talked for hours.
8 I arrived early and had a hot dog.

2 **Write the verbs into the correct column and then write the past form.**

~~follow~~ give
change eat
carry try
leave wait
notice stop
do take
push put
know see

regular		irregular	
verb	past form	verb	past form
follow	followed		

3 **Unscramble the letters and read the beginning of the story.**

1 It was midnight and the telephone *gran.* — .....rang........
2 I *rehad* it and picked it up. — ....
3 It *saw* a man. — ....
4 He *adh* a strange voice. — ....
5 He *dolt* me to go to the park. — ....
6 I *tefl* the house. — ....
7 I *newt* to the park. — ....
8 I *tem* the man. — ....
9 He *vage* me a box. — ....
10 Then he *nar* away. — ....

4 **Split the wordsnake into the past tense forms of eight verbs.**

putheldsaidsawwascarriedsattook

5 **Use the words from ④ to complete the end of the story.**

1 I ......*held*...... the box in my hands.

2 I .... it home.

3 I .... it on the table.

4 I .... down.

5 I .... the lid* off the box

6 I .... a beautiful scarf inside.

7 There .... also a note.

8 It .... 'Happy Birthday' from dad.

lid — Deckel

6 **Read the left side of the table and write the times under the pictures.**

On Sundays Allan usually:	but yesterday he:
1 gets up at 10 a.m.	got up at 9 a.m.
2 has breakfast at 10.15 a.m.	.... breakfast at 9.15 a.m.
3 runs around the park at 11 a.m.	.... around the park at 10 a.m.
4 eats lunch at 1 p.m.	.... lunch at midday.
5 meets his friend at 2 p.m.	.... his friend at 1 p.m.
6 leaves his friend's house at 6 p.m.	.... his friend's house at 5 p.m.
7 does his homework at 8 p.m.	.... his homework at 7 p.m.
8 goes to bed at 9.30 p.m.	.... to bed at 8.30 p.m.
	Why?

7 **Now complete the right side table and then answer the question. Check below to see if you were right.**

Answer: Yesterday the clocks went back but Allan forgot to change his.

51

8 **Complete the story with the past forms of the verbs.**

Somebody [1] ..followed.. (follow) Jack all the way home. What [2] .... (be) it? A man? A dog? An alien? Jack [3] .... (hurry) and then he [4] .... (run) the last 50 m to his door. Jack [5] .... (open) the front door and [6] .... (walk) inside just as the storm [7] .... (start). He [8] .... (be) happy to be home. It [9] .... (be) very dark and cold outside. It [10] .... (be) warm inside. He [11] .... (make) a cup of coffee and [12] .... (sit) down on his big red sofa. He [13] .... (turn) on the TV. Channel 1 – a man on a sofa in front of the TV, boring. He [14] .... (change) the channel. Channel 2 – the same thing; a man on a sofa in front of the TV. That [15] .... (be) strange. Channel 3 – the same again. Channel 4, 5, 6. … Jack [16] .... (take) out his phone to call his friend. He [17] .... (notice)

that the man on the TV [18] .... (do) the same thing. Jack [19] .... (get) up. The man on the TV [20] .... (get) up too. He [21] .... (sit) down again and the TV man [22] .... (sit) down too. Jack [23] .... (wave) at the TV, the man [24] .... (wave) back. And then Jack [25] .... (know). The man on the TV [26] .... (be) him. The 'TV Jack' [27] .... (turn) around. Jack [28] .... (watch) and [29] .... (see) there was somebody in the house with 'TV Jack'. Then Jack [30] .... (hear) a noise in his house. He [31] .... (turn) around too. He [32] .... (be) not alone.

9 **Use words from the three columns to write 12 sentences about the story in 8 .**

Jack Someone It	follow be run make sit turn on change wave hear	to his front door. warm inside. a cup of coffee. channels. at the man on the TV. a noise in the house. happy to be home. in the house. Jack home. on the sofa. the TV. cold outside.

Jack ran to his front door.

....

....

....

....

....

....

....

10 **Complete the sentences so that they are true about you.**

Yesterday, I …

1 (get up) ..got up at 8 a.m. ....

2 (watch) ....

3 (eat) ....

4 (be) ....

5 (meet) ....

6 (do) ....

7 (ring) ....

8 (go to bed) ....

And now go to the CD-ROM and do the *Cartoon for Fun!*

Linking words (*and, but, because*)

Mit Wörtern wie **and**, **but** und **because** kannst du Sätze miteinander verbinden.

We went to the cinema	**and** watched a great film.
	but it was closed.
	because we had free tickets.

① Match the pictures and the sentences.

1 The test was easy and I felt happy.
2 I went to bed because I was tired.
3 I ate everything and felt sick.
4 I turned off the TV and read a book.
5 I went to bed but I wasn't tired.
6 The test was easy but I forgot everything.
7 I ate everything because it was delicious.
8 I turned on the TV because I was bored.

② Match the sentence halves. Draw lines.

1 We got a taxi to the station because
2 I wanted to speak to her but
3 I turned off the TV and
4 He fell over and
5 I was excited because
6 It was raining but

a her phone was broken.
b broke his leg.
c we still went to the beach.
d it was my birthday.
e we had three big suitcases.
f went to bed.

③ Underline the correct word.

1 I don't want Paul at my party *because* / *and* I don't like him.
2 I don't like Paul *because* / *and* I don't want him at my party.
3 Mum gave me a sandwich *but* / *because* I wasn't hungry.
4 I wasn't hungry *but* / *because* I felt sick.
5 He left the house *and* / *but* went for a walk.
6 I went for a walk *and* / *but* it was too cold and I went back home.
7 I opened the window *and* / *because* I was hot.
8 I was hot *and* / *because* I opened the window.

4 Complete the sentences with *and*, *but* and *because*. Use each word once with every set of sentences.

1 He went to the shop …

.... bought an ice cream.

.... it was closed.

.... he wanted to get some milk.

2 We watched the film …

.... then went for some dinner.

.... we had nothing to do.

.... we thought it was boring.

3 I held her hand …

.... I like her.

.... kissed her.

.... I don't really like her.

4 I ordered a big pizza …

.... I was really hungry.

.... ate all of it.

.... it wasn't very good.

5 I bought the book …

.... read it in one day.

.... I never read it.

.... I really enjoyed the film.

6 I ran to the bus stop …

.... I missed the bus.

.... jumped on the bus.

.... I was late.

7 He sat down on the sofa …

.... read a book.

.... it wasn't very comfortable.

.... he was tired.

8 I rang Jenny …

.... she wasn't at home.

.... invited her to my party.

.... I needed to talk to her.

5 Complete the story with *but*, *because* or *and*.

I phoned Anne at home ¹..becaused.. I wanted to invite her to the cinema later that day. The phone rang ²...................... nobody answered it. 'Try her mobile' my mum said.

'I can't ³...................... I haven't got her number'.

'Call Tom ⁴...................... ask him' said mum.

I called Tom ⁵...................... he didn't know her number. Great! I turned on my computer ⁶...................... I wanted to send her invitation by email. ⁷...................... there was a problem with the phone line ⁸...................... I couldn't* send my invitation.

I decided to cycle to her house. I was tired when I got there ⁹...................... she lives 8 km from my house. I knocked on the door ¹⁰...................... nobody came. I left a note on her door ¹¹...................... cycled home. It started to rain ¹²...................... I got really wet.

Anne wasn't at the cinema ¹³...................... on Monday at school I asked her what happened.

'What cinema?' she asked.

'I left a note on your door.' I told her.

'Oh, that. The rain washed away the writing ¹⁴...................... I couldn't read anything.'

> *I couldn't — ich konnte nicht

And now go to the CD-ROM and do the *Cartoon for Fun!*

Past simple – negation with *did*

Hello! See me on the CD-ROM to discover more about *past simple – negation with did* and to learn better when to use it.

Verneinungen im *past simple* bildest du mit dem Hilfsverb **did not** (Kurzform: **didn't**).
Wichtig: Das *past* wird durch **didn't** ausgedrückt, das Verb folgt daher in der Grundform.

I/he/she/we/they **didn't** enjoy the film.

You **didn't** phone me.

It **didn't** rain yesterday.

1 Read the sentences. Are they about the past or the present?

1 I didn't sleep well. ....past........
2 Bob didn't do his homework. ....
3 Sue doesn't like horror films. ....
4 I don't understand the question. ....

5 We didn't play tennis. ....
6 They don't know George. ....
7 He didn't close the door again. ....
8 James didn't eat his breakfast. ....

2 Tick the correct sentence for each picture.

❶
☐ The cat liked the milk.
☑ The cat didn't like the milk.

❷
☐ He ate his peas.
☐ He didn't eat his peas.

❸
☐ He had a bad dream.
☐ He didn't have a bad dream.

❹
☐ He rescued us.
☐ He didn't rescue us.

❺
☐ He thought it was funny.
☐ He didn't think it was funny.

❻
☐ He caught the ball.
☐ He didn't catch the ball.

❼
☐ She went to school today.
☐ She didn't go to school today.

❽
☐ She enjoyed the party.
☐ She didn't enjoy the party.

3 Underline the correct word.

1 Sam didn't *like* / *liked* the party.
2 She didn't *have* / *had* a new dress to wear.
3 Tom didn't *talk* / *talked* to her.
4 She didn't *danced* / *dance* with Tom.

5 She didn't even *sat* / *sit* next to Tom.
6 She didn't *liked* / *like* the food.
7 She didn't *knew* / *know* many people.
8 She didn't *stay* / *stayed* very late.

4 **Change the sentences to make them positive and complete the poem.**

Why can't you watch TV? Why?

Well ...

You didn't feed the cat.	That's not right.
	I I fed the cat.
You didn't do your homework.	**2** ....
You didn't eat your dinner.	**3** ....
You didn't wear your hat.	**4** ....
You didn't clean your bike.	**5** ....
You didn't help your mother.	**6** ....
You didn't walk the dog.	**7** ....
You didn't play with your brother.	**8** ....
That's why.	You just didn't see.

5 **Complete the sentences with the negative forms of the verbs.**

He ...... *didn't take* ......
(take) his helmet.

He ....
(go) on the road.

He ....
(ring) his bell.

He ....
(stop) at the red light.

He ....
(hear) the policeman.

He ....
(see) the sign.

He ....
(notice) the tree.

He ....
(ride) his bike again.

6 **Match the sentences and the pictures.**

1 They caught the bus.

2 I didn't find my watch.

3 They finished their dinner.

4 I didn't get a lot of presents.

5 They didn't finish their dinner.

6 I got lots of presents.

7 They didn't catch the bus.

8 I found my watch.

7 **Complete the dialogue with the phrases in the box.**

didn't go	
you didn't	
didn't see	
I didn't know	
didn't read	
I didn't	
bought you	
Were you	
didn't look	
bought	

Jenny Happy birthday, brother. Open it.
Paul The new Seal CD. Hmmm.
Jenny What's the matter? Don't you like it?
Paul ¹.................................... in my room last week?
Jenny No, I ².................................... in your room last week. Why?
Paul And you didn't look on my desk.
Jenny No, I ³.................................... on your desk.
Paul And ⁴.................................... open my diary.
Jenny No, I ⁵.................................... your diary.
Paul And you ⁶.................................... my birthday list in it.
Jenny No, ⁷.................................... you had a birthday list.

Paul So you didn't know that I wanted the new *Vampire Weekend* CD.
Jenny No, ⁸.................................... know that you wanted that.
Paul And that's why you ⁹.................................... this Seal CD.
Jenny Yes. That's why I ¹⁰.................................... the Seal CD.
Paul Well, I hate Seal. Next year remember to look in my secret diary.
Jenny Paul, you're weird!

8 **Complete the sentences with the negative form of the verbs.**

1 They liked the new Bourne film but they ....*didn't like*............. the new James Bond.
2 She invited my brother to her party but she .... me!
3 I saw Fred at the party but I .... his girlfriend.
4 We enjoyed the book but we .... the film.
5 You said you were wrong but you .... sorry.
6 I watched the news but I .... the film after it.
7 We went to the shopping centre but we .... to the cinema.
8 He ate the broccoli but he .... the carrots.

9 **Complete the sentences with the negative forms of the verbs in the box.**

ring
~~know~~
eat
want
sleep
help
watch
buy

❶ He ....*didn't know*......... what it was.

❷ She .... all of the film.

❸ He .... to play football, I think.

❹ It .... the doorbell.

❺ We .... very well.

❻ She .... the sandwich I made for her.

❼ They .... the old lady.

❽ He .... anything.

Complete the story with the past forms of the verbs.

Once upon a time a neighbour [1]........found........ (find)
Nasruddin in his garden.

'What are you doing in my garden?' the neighbour
[2].. (ask) Nasruddin.

Nasruddin [3].. (not hear) his
neighbour so his neighbour [4]..
(speak) again.

This time Nasruddin [5].. (hear) his neighbour.

'I'm sorry', he said. 'I am looking for my key.'

His neighbour [6].. (offer) to help him. They [7].. (look)
everywhere but they [8].. (not find) the key.

'Are you sure you [9].. (drop) your key in my garden?' the neighbour said.

'Oh no.' replied Nasruddin. 'I [10].. (lose) the key in my garden.'

'But why are you looking in my garden?' [11].. (ask) the neighbour.

'Because there is more light in your garden,' Nasruddin [12].. (tell) him.

---

11 Use the verbs in the box in the past tense to complete the story.

put
ask
not clean
see
dig
arrive
say
not want
~~decide~~
not like
not
  understand
shout

Once upon a time Nasruddin [1]..........decided.......... to build a pond in his garden. He
[2].. a big hole and [3].. all the dirt* on the road outside
his neighbour's house. His neighbour wasn't happy. He [4].. the mess and
he didn't want it outside his house. He [5].. Nasruddin to clean up the
dirt. Nasruddin [6].. . He didn't think the road was a mess and he
[7].. up the dirt. The next day his neighbour asked him again. He was
very angry now and Nasruddin was a bit nervous. He [8].. to fight his
neighbour and he promised* to clean up the mess.

The next day when he [9]..
home, the neighbour [10]..
Nasruddin in the middle of a new big hole.
'What are you doing? Are you crazy?' his
neighbour [11].. 'Why are
you digging another hole?' 'I'm digging this
hole,' Nasruddin [12].. , 'to
put the dirt from the other hole in.'

dirt — Erde *promise* — versprechen

(be) going to

Wenn du ausdrücken möchtest, was jemand für die Zukunft plant oder vor hat, verwendest du eine Form von **be going to** + ein Verb in der Grundform.

I **am**		play football.
You **are**		watch a film.
He **is** / She **is**	**going to**	study.
We **are**		visit our grandparents.
You **are**		be late.
They **are**		have dinner.

1 **Match the sentences and the pictures.**

1 What are you going to do?
2 We're going to wash the dog.
3 I'm going to have a bath.
4 They're going to climb to the top.
5 What are you going to watch?
6 Is he going to jump?
7 You're going to be late.
8 It's going to rain.
9 What are we going to eat tonight?
10 She's going to win.

bungee jumping

2 **Renata is getting ready to go on holiday. Look at the picture.**
Mark the sentences T (*True*) or F (*False*).

1 Renata's going to have a holiday in Spain. [F]
2 She's going to travel by train. ☐
3 She's going to take photographs. ☐
4 She's going to take her laptop. ☐
5 She's going to stay at a campsite. ☐

6 She's going to learn Italian. ☐
7 She's going to buy some shoes for her father. ☐
8 She's going to be on holiday for two weeks. ☐

3 **Read the conversation between Renata and her friend Sam. Complete each space with the correct form of *be going to*.**

Sam Where are you going on your holiday, Renata?

Renata I ¹......*'m going to*...... visit Rome. I'm really excited. It's my first time in another country.

Sam ²........................... you .... travel by train?

Renata No, we ³........................... fly.

Sam We?

Renata Yes — my friend Sandra ⁴........................... come with me.

Sam Oh right. Where ⁵........................... you .... stay?

Renata Well, we ⁶........................... stay in a hotel — but it's a very cheap hotel because we haven't got a lot of money! But I think it ⁷........................... be OK there.

Sam And ⁸........................... you and Sandra .... share* a room?

Renata Yes — it ⁹........................... be fun, I think!

Sam Yes, I'm sure it is. And ¹⁰........................... you .... take lots of photos?

Renata Of course — you know I love photography. And when we come back, I ¹¹........................... show you all the photos — hundreds of them!

Sam Oh, great — I think!

*share — teilen

4 Put the words in order. Write the dialogues.

1 What / going / to / tomorrow / are / you / do

A _What are you going to do tomorrow?_ .... ?

going / wash / I'm / to / car / my dad's

B ....

2 you / to / Are / play / going / with us / football

A .... ?

No / going / I'm / aunt and uncle / to / visit / my

B No, ...

3 watch / you / going / to / a / Are / DVD

A .... ?

Yes / my favourite film / watch / going / I'm / to

B Yes, ...

4 your parents / Are / for your birthday / a / give you / going / bicycle / to

A .... ?

No / a / going / new / give me / they're / to / laptop

B No, ...

5 going / to / on / What / are / you / do / Sunday

A .... ?

We're / to / river / in / swim / going / the

B ....

5 Follow the lines and write the sentences. Use verbs from the box.

John   Pauline   Gran   Tommy and Angie   The dog   We

climb
play
cook
swim
drink
~~write~~

1 John _'s going to write an email._ ....

2 Pauline ....

3 Gran ....

4 Tommy and Angie ....

5 The dog ....

6 We ....

6 **Fill in the spaces. Use *going to* and a verb from the box.**

come
cook
do
eat
listen
stay
think
~~visit~~
watch

Mum Dad and I ¹......*are going to visit*...... Gran and Granddad this afternoon. But you two ²................................. here, OK?

Julia Oh mum — really?

Mike Great — I ³................................. to my favourite music — really loud!

Mum What ⁴................................. you .... , Julia?

Julia I'm not sure. I ⁵................................. about it.

Mike Huh! She ⁶................................. romantic films on DVD — I know she is!

Julia Not true!

Mike Yes it is!

Mum OK you two — quiet! Now listen. Dad and I ⁷................................. home at about eight o'clock.

Mike Eight? That's late. What about our dinner?

Mum No problem! You can make dinner tonight!

Julia OK! I ⁸................................. spaghetti.

Mike Oh no — not again!

Julia Yes, Mike — and you ⁹................................. it, OK?

Mum Bye, kids!

7 **Write sentences. What is going to happen in each picture?**

He *'s going to clean his bicycle.*

She ....

They ....

They ....

It ....

And now go to the CD-ROM and do the *Cartoon for Fun!*

Appendix

TENSES (ZEITEN)

PRESENT TENSE

Present simple (Einfache Gegenwartsform)

Die Form des *Present simple* ist für alle Personen gleich.
Ausnahme: In der 3. Person Singular wird ein **-s** angehängt.

Positive Aussagen	Negative Ausagen	Fragen	Kurzantworten	
I **like** London.	I **don't (do not) like** London.	**Do/Don't** I **like** London?	Yes, I **do**.	No, I **don't**.
You **like** London.	You **don't (do not) like** London.	**Do/Don't** you **like** London?	Yes, you **do**.	No, you **don't**.
He **likes** London.	He **doesn't (does not) like** London.	**Does/Doesn't** he **like** London?	Yes, he **does**.	No, he **doesn't**.
She **likes** London.	She **doesn't (does not) like** London.	**Does/Doesn't** she **like** London?	Yes, she **does**.	No, she **doesn't**.
It **likes** fish.	It **doesn't (does not) like** fish.	**Does/Doesn't** it **like** fish?	Yes, it **does**.	No, it **doesn't**.
We **like** London.	We **don't (do not) like** London.	**Do/Don't** we **like** London?	Yes, we **do**.	No, we **don't**.
You **like** London.	You **don't (do not) like** London.	**Do/Don't** you **like** London?	Yes, you **do**.	No, you **don't**.
They **like** London.	They **don't (do not) like** London.	**Do/Don't** they **like** London?	Yes, they **do**.	No, they **don't**.

Present continuous / present progressive (Verlaufsform, *-ing*-Form)

Das *Present continuous* wird gebildet mit der richtigen Form von **be** und der **-ing**-Form des Vollverbs.

Positive Aussagen	Negative Aussagen	Fragen	Kurzantworten	
I'm (I am) **playing** football.	I'm **not (I am not) playing** football.	Am I **playing** football?	Yes, I **am**.	No, I'm **not**.
You're (You are) **playing** football.	You **aren't (You're not) playing** football.	Are you **playing** football?	Yes, you **are**.	No, you **aren't**./No, **you're not**.
He's (He is) **playing** football.	He **isn't (He's not) playing** football.	Is he **playing** football?	Yes, he **is**.	No, he **isn't**./No, **he's not**.
She's (She is) **playing** football.	She **isn't (She's not) playing** football.	Is she **playing** football?	Yes, she **is**.	No, she **isn't**./No, **she's not**.
It's (It is) **raining**.	It **isn't (It's not) raining**.	Is it **raining**?	Yes it **is**.	No, it **isn't**./No, **it's not**.
We're (We are) **playing** football.	We **aren't (We're not) playing** football.	Are we **playing** football?	Yes, we **are**.	No we **aren't**./No, **we're not**.
You're (We are) **playing** football.	You **aren't (We're not) playing** football.	Are you **playing** football?	Yes, you **are**.	No you **aren't**./No, **you're not**.
They're (They are) **playing** football.	They **aren't (They're not) playing** football.	Are they **playing** football?	Yes, they **are**.	No, they **aren't**./No, **they're not**.

PAST TENSE

Past simple – *was / were* (einfache Vergangenheitsform)

Das *Past simple* wird bei regelmäßigen Verben mit **-ed** gebildet (siehe „regular verbs"), bei unregelmäßigen Verben mit der zweiten Form (siehe „irregular verbs").

Positive Aussage	Negative Aussage	Fragen	Kurzantworten	
I **was** tired.	I **wasn't (was not)** tired.	**Was/Wasn't** I tired?	Yes, I **was**.	No, I **wasn't (was not)**.
You **were** tired.	You **weren't (were not)** tired.	**Were/Weren't** you tired?	Yes, you **were**.	No, you **weren't (were not)**.
He **was** tired.	He **wasn't (was not)** tired.	**Was/Wasn't** he tired?	Yes, he **was**.	No, he **wasn't (was not)**.
She **was** tired.	She **wasn't (was not)** tired.	**Was/Wasn't** she tired?	Yes, she **was**.	No, she **wasn't (was not)**.
It **was** blue.	It **wasn't (was not)** blue.	**Was/Wasn't** it blue?	Yes, it **was**.	No, it **wasn't (was not)**.
We **were** tired.	We **weren't (were not)** tired.	**Were/Weren't** we tired?	Yes, we **were**.	No, we **weren't (were not)**.
You **were** tired.	You **weren't (were not)** tired.	**Were/Weren't** you tired?	Yes, you **were**.	No, you **weren't (were not)**.
They **were** tired.	They **weren't (were not)** tired.	**Were/Weren't** they tired?	Yes, they **were**.	No, they **weren't (were not)**.

Regular verbs (Regelmäßige Verben)

Positive Aussage	Negative Aussage
I lik**ed** London.	I **didn't (did not) like** London.
You laugh**ed** a lot.	You **didn't (did not) laugh** a lot.
He walk**ed** home.	He **didn't (did not) walk** home.
She look**ed** good.	She **didn't (did not) look** good.
It turn**ed** around.	It **didn't (did not) turn** around.
We cook**ed** dinner.	We **didn't (did not) cook** dinner.
You cook**ed** dinner.	You **didn't (did not) cook** dinner.
They lov**ed** the film.	They **didn't (did not) love** the film.

Irregular verbs (Unregelmäßige Verben)

Hier findest du eine Liste mit einer Auswahl der wichtigsten unregelmäßigen Verben.

Present tense	Past simple tense	Übersetzung	Present tense	Past simple tense	Übersetzung
be	was/were	*sein*	know	knew	*wissen, kennen*
become	became	*werden*	learn	learnt	*lernen*
begin	began	*beginnen*	leaves	left	*verlassen*
blow	blew	*blasen*	let	let	*lassen*
break	broke	*brechen*	lose	lost	*verlieren*
build	built	*bauen*	make	made	*machen*
buy	bought	*kaufen*	meet	met	*treffen*
catch	caught	*fangen*	put	put	*geben, setzen, stellen*
choose	chose	*wählen*	read	read	*lesen*
come	came	*kommen*	ride	rode	*reiten, fahren*
cut	cut	*schneiden*	ring	rang	*läuten*
dig	dug	*graben*	run	ran	*laufen*
do	did	*tun, machen*	say	said	*sagen*
draw	drew	*zeichnen*	see	saw	*sehen*
drink	drank	*trinken*	send	sent	*senden, schicken*
drive	drove	*fahren, treiben*	sing	sang	*singen*
eat	ate	*essen*	sit	sat	*sitzen, sich setzen*
fall	fell	*fallen*	sleep	slept	*schlafen*
feel	felt	*fühlen*	speak	spoke	*sprechen, sagen*
fight	fought	*kämpfen*	spend	spent	*verbringen, ausgeben*
find	found	*finden*	stand	stood	*stehen*
fly	flew	*fliegen*	steal	stole	*stehlen*
forget	forgot	*vergessen*	swim	swam	*schwimmen*
get	got	*bekommen, werden*	take off	took off	*ausziehen*
get up	got up	*aufstehen*	take	took	*nehmen*
give	gave	*geben*	teach	taught	*lehren, unterrichten*
go	went	*gehen, fahren*	tell, tells	told	*sagen, erzählen*
have	had	*haben*	think	thought	*denken*
hear	heard	*hören*	wake (up)	woke (up)	*(auf)wachen*
hide	hid	*(sich) verstecken*	win	won	*gewinnen*
hit	hit	*schlagen*	write	wrote	*schreiben*
hold	held	*halten*			
hurt	hurt	*verletzen, schmerzen*			

FUTURE TENSE

going to-future (Zukunft mit *going to*)

Die *going-to-future* wird mit einer Form von **be** und **going to** und der Grundform des Vollverbs gebildet.

Positive Aussage		Negative Aussage		Fragen		Kurzantworten
I'm		I'm not		Am I		Yes, I **am**. / No I'm **not**.
You're		You **aren't** (You're **not**)		Are / Aren't you		Yes, you **are**. / No, you **aren't** (you're **not**).
He's		He **isn't** (He's **not**)		Is / Isn't he		Yes, he **is**. / No, he **isn't** (he's **not**).
She's	going to play football.	She **isn't** (She's **not**)	going to play football.	Is / Isn't she	going to play football?	Yes, she **is**. / No, she **isn't** (she's **not**).
We're		We **aren't** (We're **not**)		Are / Aren't we		Yes, we **are**. / No, we **aren't** / we're **not**.
You're		You **aren't** (You're **not**)		Are / Aren't you		Yes, you **are**. / No, you **aren't** / you're **not**.
They're		They **aren't** (They're **not**)		Are / Aren't they		Yes, they **are**. / No, they **aren't** / they're **not**.

BESONDERE VERBEN

to be — affirmative, negative

Das Verb **be** wird wie das deutsche Verb **sein** verwendet.

Positive Aussage	Negative Aussage
I'm (**I am**) tired.	I'm **not** tired.
You're (**You are**) clever.	You **aren't**/You're **not** tired.
He's (**He is**) nice.	He **isn't**/He's **not** nice.
She's (**She is**) in class 3B.	She **isn't**/She's **not** in class 3B.
It's (**It is**) blue.	It **isn't**/It's **not** blue.
We're (**We are**) busy.	We **aren't**/We're **not** busy.
You're (**You are**) busy.	You **aren't**/You're **not** busy.
They're (**They are**) twelve.	They **aren't**/They're **not** twelve.

Questions with *be*

Fragen	Kurzantworten	
Am I tired?	Yes, I **am**.	No, I'm **not**.
Are/Aren't you tired?	Yes, you **are**.	No, you **aren't**./No, you're **not**.
Is/Isn't he nice?	Yes, he **is**.	No, he **isn't**./No, he's **not**.
Is/Isn't she in class 3B?	Yes, she **is**.	No, she **isn't**./No, she's **not**.
Is/Isn't it blue?	Yes, it **is**.	No, it **isn't**./No, it's **not**.
Are/Aren't we busy?	Yes, we **are**.	No, we **aren't**./No, we're **not**.
Are/Aren't you busy?	Yes, you **are**.	No, you **aren't**./No, you're **not**.
Are/Aren't they twelve?	Yes, they **are**.	No, they **aren't**./No, they're **not**.

have got / haven't got

Have got wird wie das deutsche Verb **haben** (besitzen) verwendet.
Die richtige Form für die 3. Person der Gegenwarts (**he/she/it**) ist **has got**.

Positive Aussage	Negative Aussage	Fragen	Kurzantworten	
I've got (**I have got**) a dog.	I **haven't got** (have not got) a dog.	**Have/Haven't** I **got** a dog?	Yes, I **have**.	No, I **haven't**.
You've got (**You have got**) a dog.	You **haven't got** (have not got) a dog.	**Have/Haven't** you **got** a dog?	Yes, you **have**.	No, you **haven't**.
He's got (**He has got**) a dog.	He **hasn't got** (has not got) a dog.	**Has/Hasn't** he **got** a dog?	Yes, he **has**.	No, he **hasn't**.
She's got (**She has got**) a dog.	She **hasn't got** (has not got) a dog.	**Has/Hasn't** she **got** a dog?	Yes, she **has**.	No, she **hasn't**.
It's got (**It has got**) big ears.	It **hasn't got** (has not got) big ears.	**Has/Hasn't** it **got** big ears?	Yes, it **has**.	No, it **hasn't**.
We've got (**We have got**) a dog.	We **haven't got** (have not got) a dog.	**Have/Haven't** we **got** a dog?	Yes, we **have**.	No, we **haven't**.
You've got (**We have got**) a dog.	You **haven't got** (have not got) a dog.	**Have/Haven't** you **got** a dog?	Yes, you **have**.	No, you **haven't**.
They've got (**They have got**) a dog.	They **haven't got** (have not got) a dog.	**Have/Haven't** they **got** a dog?	Yes, they **have**.	No, they **haven't**.

there is / there are

There is / **there are** wird verwendet, um auszudrücken, dass etwas vorhanden ist, oder dass es etwas gibt.

There's a monster in the tree. (= **There is** a monster in the tree.)   **There are** three frogs on the table.

can / can't

Can ist ein Modalverb und wird deshalb immer in Verbindung mit einem Vollverb verwendet. Die Verneinung wird gebildet als **cannot** oder **can't**.

Positive Aussagen	Negative Aussagen	Fragen	Kurzantworten	
I **can speak** French.	I **can't** (**cannot**) **speak** French.	**Can/Can't** I speak French?	Yes, I **can.**	No, I **can't.**
You **can speak** French.	You **can't** (**cannot**) **speak** French.	**Can/Can't** you speak French?	Yes, you **can.**	No, you **can't.**
He **can speak** French.	He **can't** (**cannot**) **speak** French.	**Can/Can't** he speak French?	Yes, he **can.**	No, he **can't.**
She **can speak** French.	She **can't** (**cannot**) **speak** French.	**Can/Can't** she speak French?	Yes, she **can.**	No, she **can't.**
It **can run** fast.	It **can't** (**cannot**) **run** fast.	**Can/Can't** it run fast?	Yes, it **can.**	No, it **can't.**
We **can speak** French.	We **can't** (**cannot**) **speak** French.	**Can/Can't** we speak French?	Yes, we **can.**	No, we **can't.**
You **can speak** French.	You **can't** (**cannot**) **speak** French.	**Can/Can't** you speak French?	Yes, you **can.**	No, you **can't.**
They **can speak** French.	They **can't** (**cannot**) **speak** French.	**Can/Can't** they speak French?	Yes, they **can.**	No, they **can't.**

ADVERBS (ADVERBIEN)

Generell bildet man Adverbien, indem man an die Grundform des Adjektivs **-ly** anhängt.

| usual – usual**ly** | sad – sad**ly** | furious – furious**ly** |

Adverbs of frequency (always, often, usually, sometimes, never) (Häufigkeitsadverbien)

0%	→	→	→	100%
never	sometimes	often	usually	always

We **sometimes** go to the cinema on Fridays.
She's **always** happy.

IMPERATIVES (IMPERATIV / BEFEHLSFORMEN)

Die Befehlsform ist immer gleich wie die Grundform des Verbs (ohne **to**). Die Verneinung wird mit **do not** (**don't**) + Grundform gebildet.

Run!	Don't run!
Sit down.	Don't sit down.
Open the window.	Don't open the window.

ARTICLES (ARTIKEL)

Indefinite article (Unbestimmter Artikel)

Der unbestimmte Artikel **a** wird vor einem zählbaren Hauptwort verwendet, **an** wird vor Selbstlauten verwendet.

a bike	Vor den Vokalen (Selbstlauten): a, e, i, o, u
a teacher	**an** egg /ən ˈeg/
a dog	**an** apple /ən ˈæpl/

Definite article (Bestimmter Artikel)

Der bestimmte Artikel, verwendet wie im Deutschen **der/die/das**, ist im Englischen immer **the**.

| **the** bike | **the** teacher | **the** dog |

NOUNS (HAUPTWÖRTER)

Plural nouns – irregular plurals (Pluralformen)

Regelmäßige Pluralformen werden gebildet, indem ein **-s** angehängt wird.
Bei unregelmäßigen Formen wird am Wortende **-y** zu **-ies** (Vokal vor **-y** bleibt **-y**) und **-f** oder **-fe** zu **-ves**.

Regelmäßig		
dog – dog**s**	snake – snake**s**	cat – cat**s**

Unregelmäßig					
baby – bab**ies**	leaf – lea**ves**	li**fe** – li**ves**	child – children	mouse – mice	foot – feet

Possessive 's

Wenn man anzeigen will, das etwas jemandem gehört, hängt man an das Hauptwort ein **'s** an.

It's **John's** dog.
It's **my brother's** computer.

PRONOUNS (PRONOMEN)

Question words (Fragewörter)

Who	What	Where	How often
Who is she?	**What's** your name?	**Where** are you now?	**How often** do you go to the cinema?
Who are you?	**What** eats insects?	**Where** do you live?	
Who likes ice cream?	**What** does your dog eat?		
Who do you like?			

this / that, these / those

This / **that**, **these** / **those** sind Demonstrativpronomen, die verwendet werden, um Nähe oder Ferne auszudrücken.
This / **these** beschreibt etwas in der Nähe, **that** / **those** etwas weiter Entferntes.

I like **this** jumper here.	I like **that** jumper over there.	I like **these** shoes here.	I like **those** shoes over there.

Possessives

Possessives stehen immer vor dem Hauptwort und zeigen an, wem oder zu wem etwas gehört.

I	you	he	she	it	we	they
my	**your**	**his**	**her**	**its**	**our**	**their**

Personal pronouns / Subject and object pronouns (Personalpronomen)

Personalpronomen können als Subjekt oder Objekt eines Satzes verwendet werden.
Das unpersönliche deutsche **man** kann im Englischen durch **you**, **they** oder **one** ausgedrückt werden.

Subjekt	I	You	He	She	It	We	They
Objekt	me	you	him	her	it	us	them

PREPOSITIONS (PRÄPOSITIONEN)

Präpositionen stehen vor einem Hauptwort oder Pronomen und zeigen die Richtung, den Ort, oder die Zeit (siehe „time prepositions") an.

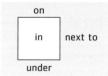

Time prepositions (*in, on, at*) (Präpositionen der Zeit)

My birthday is **on** February 12th / May 28th / September 5th.

My sister's birthday is **in** December / April / June.

The film starts **at** 7 o'clock / half past eight / six forty-five.

We have Maths **in** the morning / in the afternoon.

We go to bed late **at** night.

CONJUNCTIONS (KONJUNKTIONEN)

Linking words (*and, but, because*)

Konjunktionen verbinden Hauptsätze und Nebensätze miteinander.

We went to the cinema **and** watched a great film.

but it was closed.

because we had free tickets.

QUANTITY / MEASUREMENT (MENGENANGABEN)

How much is/are...?

Mit **how much** wird nach der Menge (bei nichtzählbaren Hauptwörtern) oder nach dem Preis gefragt.

How much ice cream do you eat every day?

How much money have you got?

How much is the ice cream?

How much are the trainers?

Ordinal numbers

Cardinal		Ordinal	Cardinal		Ordinal
1	one	**first**	16	sixteen	sixteen**th**
2	two	**second**	17	seventeen	seventeen**th**
3	three	**third**	18	eighteen	eighteen**th**
4	four	four**th**	19	nineteen	nineteen**th**
5	five	fif**th**	20	twenty	twentie**th**
6	six	six**th**	21	twenty-one	twenty-**first**
7	seven	seven**th**	30	thirty	thirtie**th**
8	eight	eigh**th**	40	forty	fortie**th**
9	nine	nin**th**	50	fifty	fiftie**th**
10	ten	ten**th**	60	sixty	sixtie**th**
11	eleven	eleven**th**	70	seventy	seventie**th**
12	twelve	twelf**th**	80	eighty	eightie**th**
13	thirteen	thirteen**th**	90	ninety	ninetie**th**
14	fourteen	fourteen**th**	100	hundred	hundred**th**
15	fifteen	fifteen**th**	101	a/one hundred and one	**the (one) hundred and first**

Wordlist

A

a	ein, eine
about	über
above	über
accident	Unfall
adult	Erwachsene/r
adventure	Abenteuer; Erlebnis
after	nach
afternoon	Nachmittag
again	wieder; noch einmal, noch mal
(two days) ago	vor (zwei Tagen)
all	alle(s)
alone	allein
aloud	laut
alphabet	Alphabet
alright	in Ordnung
also	auch
always	immer
a.m.	vormittags
ambulance	Krankenwagen
and	und
and so on	und so weiter
angry	verärgert; zornig; wütend
animal	Tier
another	noch eine(r, s); ein andere(r, s)
answer	Antwort; anworten
any	irgendein/e
any more	nicht mehr
Anything else?	Darf es noch etwas sein?
any way	auf alle Fälle
apple	Apfel
April	April
arm	Arm
around	um; herum
arrive	ankommen
as ... as ...	(genau)so ... wie ...
ask	fragen; bitten
at	bei, auf, um
at first	anfangs, zuerst
at home	zu Hause
at last	schließlich, endlich
attack	angreifen
August	August
aunty (informal)	Tantchen
authograph	Autogramm
away	weg

B

back	zurück
bad	schlecht, böse
bag	Tasche, Tüte
baked potato	Folienkartoffel
baker	Bäcker/in
ball	Ball
banana	Banane
band	Band; Kapelle
bank	Bank
bar	Stange; hier: Riegel
have a barbecue	grillen
basket	Korb

bat	Fledermaus
bathroom	Bad(ezimmer)
beach	Strand
bean	Bohne
bear	Bär
beard	Bart
beautiful	schön
because	weil
become	werden
bed	Bett
bedroom	Schlafzimmer
beef	Rindfleisch
before	bevor; zuvor; vor
begin	beginnen
beginning	Anfang
behind	hinter
believe	glauben
best	beste(r, s)
better	besser
big	groß
billion	Milliarde
bike	(Fahr)rad
binoculars	Fernglas
bird	Vogel
bird-watcher	Vogelbeobachter/in
birthday	Geburtstag
biscuit	Keks
a bit	ein wenig
bite	beißen
black	schwarz
blouse	Bluse
blue	blau
board	Tafel
boat	Boot
book	Buch
body	Körper
be bored	sich langweilen
boring	langweilig
born	geboren
both	beide
box	Schachtel, Kiste
boy	Junge
boyfriend	Freund (eines Mädchens)
branch	Zweig; Ast
bread	Brot
break	brechen
breakfast	Frühstück
bridge	Brücke
brilliant	toll; großartig
bring	(mit)bringen
broccoli	Brokkoli
brother	Bruder
brown	braun
budgie (informal)	Wellensittich
buffalo (pl buffaloes)	Büffel
building	Gebäude
bump into ...	mit ... zusammenstoßen
bus	Bus
bus stop	Bushaltestelle
bush (pl bushes)	Busch
busy	beschäftigt

but	aber
butter	Butter
butterfly	Schmetterling
buy	kaufen
by	bei, mit
bye	Tschüss!

C

cage	Käfig
cake	Kuchen
calendar	Kalender
call	rufen; anrufen
camel	Kamel
campsite	Campingplatz
can	können
can	Dose
canteen	Kantine
cap	Mütze, Kappe
capital	Hauptstadt
captain	Kapitän
car	Auto
card	Karte
careful	vorsichtig
carol	Weihnachtslied
carrot	Möhre, Karotte
carry	tragen
carry home	nach Hause tragen
case	Fall; Hülle
castle	Burg; Schloss
cat	Katze
catch	fangen; kriegen
certainly	sicher(lich); bestimmt
chair	Stuhl
change	(sich) (ver)ändern
chase	verfolgen, jagen
chat	Unterhaltung, Plauderei, Chat
check	überprüfen, kontrollieren
Cheer up!	Lass den Kopf nicht hängen!, Kopf hoch!
cheese	Käse
chicken	Huhn
child, children	Kind, Kinder
chimney	Schornstein
chips	Pommes frites
chocolate	Schokolade
choose	wählen
Christmas	Weihnachten
Christmas Eve	Heiligabend
cinema	Kino
circle	einkreisen; Kreis
city	(Groß)stadt
class	(Schul)klasse
classroom	Klassenzimmer
clean	sauber machen, reinigen, putzen
clever	klug, gescheit, schlau
climb	(hinauf)steigen; klettern
clock	Uhr
close	schließen, zumachen
close	nah, knapp
clothes (no pl)	Kleider, Kleidung

clue	Hinweis, Anhaltspunkt; Tipp
cold	kalt
collect	sammeln
colour	Farbe; anmalen
come	kommen
come along	mitgehen, mitkommen
Come on!	Komm(t) jetzt! Mach(t) schon!
complete	vervollständigen
concentrate	(sich) konzentrieren
concert	Konzert
confused	verwirrt
congratulations (no pl)	Glückwunsch, Glückwünsche
cook	kochen; Koch/Köchin
corner	Ecke
correct	korrigieren
correct	richtig, korrekt
count	zählen
country	Land; Staat
cow	Kuh
cracker	Knallbonbon
crash	stürzen
crazy	verrückt
crime	Verbrechen
crocodile	Krokodil
cry	weinen; schreien
cut	schneiden
cycling	Rad fahren, Radeln

D

dad	Papa
dance	tanzen
dare	herausfordern; sich trauen
How dare you!	Wie kannst du es wagen!
dark	Dunkelheit; dunkel
date	Datum
day	Tag
dear	lieb, teuer
December	Dezember
describe	beschreiben
desk	Schreibtisch
detective	(Privat)detektiv/in
dial	wählen
dialogue	Gespräch, Dialog
die	sterben
different	anders, andere(r, s); verschieden
difficult	schwierig, schwer
dig	graben
dining room	Esszimmer
dinner	Abendessen
dinner lady	servierende Aufseherin an Schulen
dirt	Erde
do	machen, tun
dog	Hund
done	fertig, erledigt
door	Tür
dotted	gestrichelt
double	doppelt, Doppel-
dove	Taube
down	hinunter; hinab
dragon	Drache
drawer	Schublade
dream	Traum; träumen
dress	Kleid
drink	Getränk; trinken

drive	fahren
drummer	Trommler/in, Schlagzeuger/in
drums	Schlagzeug/Trommeln
duck	Ente
during	während

E

each	jede(r, s)
eagle	Adler
ear	Ohr
early	früh
easy	einfach
eat	essen
eater	Esser/in
egg	Ei
eight	acht
eighteen	achtzehn
eighteenth	achtzehnte(r, s)
eighth	achte(r, s)
elephant	Elefant
eleven	elf
eleventh	elfte(r, s)
emergency	Notfall, Notdienst
empty	leer
end	Ende; enden
English	englisch; Englisch; Engländer/in
enjoy	genießen
enough	genug
episode	Ereignis, Vorfall, Episode
evening	Abend
every	jede(r, s)
everybody	jede(r); alle
everyday	Alltags-; für jeden Tag
everything	alles
excellent	ausgezeichnet
excited	aufgeregt
exciting	aufregend; spannend
Excuse me!	Entschuldigen Sie bitte!, Entschuldigung!
eye	Auge

F

face	Gesicht
fall	fallen
false	falsch
family	Familie
famous	berühmt
fantastic	fantastisch
fantasy	Fantasie, Fantasy
far	von weit her; weit
farm	Bauernhof
fast	schnell
father	Vater
fault	Schuld
favourite	Lieblings-
February	Februar
feed	zu essen geben, füttern
feel	(sich) fühlen
fifteen	fünfzehn
fifteenth	fünfzehnte(r, s)
fifth	fünfte(r, s)
fig	Feige
film	Film
finally	schließlich; endlich
find	finden
fine	in Ordnung, gut
finger	Finger
Finnish	finnisch; Finnisch

fire	Feuer
fireplace	Kamin
first	erste(r, s)
fish (pl fish)	Fisch, Fische
fishing	Fischen, Angeln
fishing rod	Angelrute
five	fünf
flag	Fahne; Flagge
flash	Blitz(licht)
flat	Wohnung
floor	Boden
fly	fliegen
fold	falten
folk tale	Volksmärchen
follow	folgen
be fond (of)	(etw.) gerne mögen
food (no pl)	Essen
foot (pl feet)	Fuß
football	Fußball
for	für
forget	vergessen
(You) forgot	Du hast vergessen
four	vier
fourteen	vierzehn
fourteenth	vierzehnte(r, s)
fourth	vierte(r, s)
fox (pl foxes)	Fuchs
free	befreien; frei, kostenlos
freedom	Freiheit, Unabhängigkeit
freeze	gefrieren; einfrieren
French	französisch; Französisch
Friday	Freitag
fridge (informal)	Kühlschrank
friend	Freund(in)
friendship	Freundschaft
frog	Frosch
from	von, aus
front door	Vordertür; Haustür
fruit	Frucht; Obst
full	voll
fun	Spaß
be fun	Spaß machen

G

game	Spiel
garden	Garten
German	deutsch; Deutsch
get	erhalten, bekommen; holen
get out (of)	hinauskommen/ herauskommen (aus)
get up	aufstehen
girl	Mädchen
give	geben
glasses	Brille
glue	Klebstoff
glue stick	Klebestift
gnome	(Garten-)Zwerg
go	gehen, laufen
Go ahead!	Aber bitte!
go on	weitergehen; weitermachen
go to bed	ins Bett / zu Bett gehen
go to sleep	schlafen gehen
golden	aus Gold, golden
good	gut
goodbye	auf Wiedersehen
goose (pl geese)	Gans
gosh (informal)	Oh Mann! Mensch!
grandfather	Großvater

grandma	Oma, Omi
grandmother	Großmutter
grandpa	Opa, Opi
grass	Gras
great	groß, riesig; großartig, wunderbar
Greek	griechisch; Griechisch
green	grün
grey	grau
ground	(Erd)boden, Erde
guess	(er)raten
guest	Gast
guinea pig	Meerschweinchen
guitar	Gitarre
guitarist	Gitarist
guy	Kerl

H

hair (no pl)	Haar(e)
half (pl halves)	halb
half past (three)	halb (vier)
hall	Korridor; Halle
hand	Hand
hang up	aufhängen
happen	geschehen, passieren
happy	glücklich; zufrieden; fröhlich
hat	Hut
hate	hassen, nicht ausstehen können
have	haben
have got	haben
have to	müssen
hay	Heu
he	er
head	Kopf
hear	hören
heaven	Himmel
helicopter	Hubschrauber
hello	hallo
help	Hilfe; helfen
her	ihr(e, em, en)
here	hier, her
Here we go!	Jetzt geht's los!
Here you are.	Hier, bitte!/Bitte schön!
Hi there.	Hallo ihr!
hide	(sich) verstecken
him	ihm, ihn
hippo (= hippo- potamus)	Nilpferd
hire	mieten, ausleihen
his	sein(e, r)
hit	schlagen (auf)
hold	(fest)halten
hold up	nach oben halten
hole	Loch
holiday	Urlaub, Ferien
home	zu/nach Hause, Zuhause
homework (no pl)	Hausaufgaben
honey	Honig
hook	Haken
hop	Hüpfer
hope	hoffen
horror	Entsetzen, Grauen, Horror
horse	Pferd
horsey	hier: Pferdchen
hospital	Krankenhaus
hot	heiß
hour	Stunde

house	Haus
how	wie
How are you?	Wie geht es dir Ihnen/euch?
How many?	Wieviele?
How much?	Wieviele?
hundred	Hundert
hungry	hungrig
hunt	Jagd; jagen
hurry	sich beeilen
hurry up	sich beeilen
hurt	wehtun, schmerzen; schaden
husband	Ehemann
hut	Hütte

I

I	ich
I'm (I am)	ich bin; ich heiße
I'm fine.	Es geht mir gut.
I'm hot.	Mir ist heiß.
I'm sorry.	Das tut mir leid.
ice cream	Eiscreme
idea	Idee
ill	krank
in	in, hinein, im
indoors	drinnen
in front of	vor
in one go	auf einmal
in pairs	paarweise
insect	Insekt
inside	innen; hinein
inspector	Inspektor/in
instruction	Anweisung
instrument	Instrument
interesting	interessant
into	in
invite	einladen
island	Insel
it	es
Italian	italienisch; Italienisch
its	sein(e), ihr(e)
It's a shame.	Das ist schade.
It's me.	Ich bin's.
It's yours.	Es gehört dir.

J

jackal	Schakal
jacket	Jacke
January	Januar
job	Arbeit, Stelle, Tätigkeit, Aufgabe
join (in)	teilnehmen (an), mitmachen (bei)
join hands	sich die Hände geben
joke	Scherz
juggle	jonglieren
juice	Saft
July	Juli
jump	springen
June	Juni
junk food	Schnellgerichte; ungesundes Essen
just	nur; gerade
Just a minute/ moment.	Einen Augenblick/ Moment bitte.
Just kidding!	War nur ein Scherz.

K

keep	(be)halten
key	Schlüssel, Taste

key-ring	Schlüsselanhänger
kid	Kind
kill	töten
kilo	Kilo
kilometre	Kilometer
what kind (of)	was für
king	König
kitchen	Küche
knee	Knie
knock	Klopfen; klopfen
know	wissen; kennen

L

lady	Frau; Dame
land	landen
language	Sprache
last	letzte(r, s)
late	(zu) spät
later	später
laugh	lachen
laughter	Gelächter
lazy	faul; träge
leaf (pl leaves)	Blatt
learn	lernen
leave	verlassen, weggehen
left	linke(r, s)
leg	Bein
lesson	(Unterrichts)stunde
let	lassen
let go	loslassen
let's (= let us)	lass(t) uns
Let's go!	Los! Gehen wir!
letter	Buchstabe; Brief
library	Bibliothek, Bücherei
lid	Deckel
lie	liegen; sich legen
life (pl lives)	Leben
lift (up)	(hoch)heben
like	mögen
like ...	so wie ...
lion	Löwe
listen	zuhören
a little	ein bisschen
little	klein
live	leben
living room	Wohnzimmer
long	lang
look	sehen, schauen; aussehen
look after	sich kümmern um
look at	betrachten, sehen
look for	suchen nach
Lord	Lord; Herr
a lot (of)	viel(e)
lots of	viel, jede Menge
loud	laut
love	Liebe; lieben, mögen
lovely	schön, hübsch
lucky	glücklich
be lucky	Glück haben
lucky charm	Glücksbringer
lunch	Mittagessen

M

macaroni	Makkaroni
mad	wahnsinnig; böse
madam	gnädige Frau
magazine	Zeitschrift, Magazin
maid	Dienstmädchen
make	machen

man (pl men)	Mann	nineteen	neunzehn	pet	Haustier
many	viele	ninth	neunte(r, s)	phone	Telefon; anrufen
March	März	no	nein; kein	phrase	Redewendung, Satzteil
master	Herr; Meister	No way!	Auf keinen Fall!	piano	Klavier; Piano
mat	Matte	nobody	niemand	pick up	aufheben, abholen
match	Match, Spiel	noise	Lärm, Krach; Geräusch	picture	Bild
Maths	Mathe(matik)	noodle	Nudel	piece	Stück
It doesn't matter.	Das ist nicht wichtig.	nose	Nase	piggy bank	Sparschwein
May	Mai	not	nicht	pilot	Pilot/in
maybe	vielleicht	nothing	nichts	pink	rosa, pink
me	mir, mich: ich	notice	bemerken	pirate	Pirat/in, Seeräuber/in
(it's) me	Ich bin es.	November	November	place	Ort; Platz; Wohnung
meet	(sich) treffen, kennenlernen	now	jetzt	play	spielen
		number	Zahl; Ziffer; Nummer	player	Spieler/in, Player
message	Nachricht			playground	Spielplatz
messy	unordentlich, schlampig			please	bitte
microwave	Mikrowelle(nherd)	**O**		p.m.	nachmittags, abends (nur hinter Uhrzeit zwischen 12 Uhr mittags und Mitternacht)
midday	Mittag	(five) o'clock	(fünf) Uhr		
middle	Mitte	October	Oktober		
midnight	Mitternacht	of	von		
milk	Milch	of course	natürlich		
mime	mimen	off	aus; weg	poem	Gedicht
minute	Minute	often	oft, häufig	point	Punkt
miss	Frau, Fräulein	Oh dear!	Du meine Güte!	police (no pl)	Polizei
missing	fehlend	old	alt	policeman, -men	Polizist, Polizisten
mistake	Fehler	on	auf, an, am	Polish	polnisch; Polnisch
mobile (phone)	Mobiltelefon, Handy	be on fire	brennen, in Flammen stehen	pond	Teich
moment	Moment, Augenblick			pony (pl ponies)	Pony
Monday	Montag	once	einmal	poor	arm
money	Geld	once upon a time	es war einmal	postcard	Postkarte
month	Monat	one	eins; ein(e)	potato (pl potatoes)	Kartoffel
more	mehr	onion	Zwiebel		
morning	Morgen	only	nur	pound (£)	Pfund
morph	sich verwandeln	onto	auf	practice	Übung
mother	Mutter	open	(sich) öffnen	practise	üben
mouse (pl mice)	Maus	or	oder	prefect	Aufsichtsperson
mouth	Mund	orange	Orange; orange(farbig)	prepare	vorbereiten
Mr	Herr (Anrede)	order	Reihenfolge	present	Geschenk
Mrs	Frau (Anrede)	our	unser(e)	pretty	hübsch
much	viel; sehr	out	heraus, nach draußen	price	Preis
mum	Mama, Mutti	out of	aus	prince	Prinz
music	Musik	outside	außen, außerhalb	problem	Problem
must	müssen	over	über; herüber	programme	Programm, Sendung
my	mein(e)	owl	Eule	project	Projekt
		own	eigene(r, s)	projector	Projektor
N		owner	Besitzer/in, Eigentümer/in	promise	Versprechen
name	Name			proud	stolz
What's your name?	Wie heißt du?, Wie heißen Sie?			pudding (Christmas)	englische Süßspeise
		P			
nationality	Nationalität	packed lunch	Jausenbrot	pull	ziehen
nature	Natur	paintbrush	Pinsel	purple	violett, lila
near	nahe bei	a pair of	ein Paar (von)	push	schieben
need	brauchen	in pairs	zu Zweit	put	hineinstecken, hineintun
neighbour	Nachbar/in	paper	Papier; hier: Zeitung		
nervous	nervös	parents (pl)	Eltern	put	legen, stellen
nest	Nest	park	Park	puzzle	Rätsel
net	Netz	parrot	Papagei		
never	nie(mals)	past	nach	**Q**	
new	neu	pasta (no pl)	Nudeln, Teigwaren	quack	quaken
news (pl)	Nachrichten	pea	Erbse	quarter	Viertel(stunde)
newsagent's	Zeitungsgeschäft	peace	Friede	question	Frage
newspaper	Zeitung	pelican	Pelikan	quick	schnell
next	nächste(r,s)	pen	Feder; Stift	quickly	schnell
next to	neben	pence (p)	Pence	quiet	leise, ruhig
nice	schön, angenehm	pencil	Bleistift	quite	ziemlich
Nice to meet you!	Es freut mich, Sie/dich kennen zulernen.	pencil case	Federmäppchen	quiz (pl quizzes)	Quiz, Ratespiel
		pencil sharpener	(Bleistift)spitzer		
at night	nachts; hier: am Abend	people (pl)	Leute, Menschen	**R**	
night	Nacht, Abend	pepper	Pfeffer; hier: Paprika	rabbit	Kaninchen
nine	neun	perfect	perfekt	race	Rasse
		perhaps	vielleicht	rain	Regen; regnen

rat	Ratte	seven	sieben	squirrel	Eichhörnchen
reaction	Reaktion	seventeen	siebzehn	stand	stehen
read	lesen	seventeenth	siebzehnte(r; s)	stand up (for)	sich einsetzen (für)
ready	fertig	seventh	siebte(r; s)	staple	klammern
real	wirklich; echt	shape	Form	start	anfangen
really	wirklich	share	teilen	stay	bleiben
red	rot	shark	Hai(fisch)	stay up late	lang aufbleiben
reindeer	Rentier	she	sie	step	Schritt
remember	sich erinnern (an)	shed	Schuppen, Stall	stick	kleben; Stock
republic	Republik	ship	Schiff	stocking	Strumpf
rescue	retten; Rettung	shirt	Hemd	stone	Stein
rest	Rest	shoe	Schuh	stop	Halt; hier: Haltestelle; stoppen, anhalten, aufhören
return	zurückkehren, zurückkommen	shop	Geschäft, Laden		
		shopping	Einkaufen	Stop it!	Hör auf, hören Sie auf (damit)!
rhyme	Reim	short	kurz, klein		
rice	Reis	shoulder	Schulter	storm	Sturm
rich	reich	shout	schreien, rufen	story	Geschichte, Erzählung
ride	Ritt; Fahrt; reiten, fahren	show	zeigen	strange	sonderbar
right	richtig; rechte(r; s)	shut down	herunterfahren	street	Straße
be right	Recht haben	(feel) sick	sich schlecht fühlen	strip	Streifen
ring	Ring; klingeln, läuten, anrufen	signal	Empfang; Signal	stripe	Streifen
		silly	albern, dumm	strong	stark
river	Fluss	sing	singen	strongest	stärkste(r;s)
road	Straße	singer	Sänger/in	suddenly	plötzlich, auf einmal
roast	Brat-; gebraten	sir	Herr (Anrede)	summer	Sommer
robber	Räuber	sister	Schwester	Sunday	Sonntag
robbery	Raubüberfall	sit	sitzen, sich hinsetzen	sunny	sonnig
rock	schaukeln, rocken; Rock(musik); Stein, Fels	sit down	sich (hin)setzen	sunshine	Sonnenschein
		six	sechs	sure	sicher
romantic	romantisch	sixteen	sechzehn	surprise	Überraschung
roof	Dach	sixteenth	sechzehnte(r; s)	sweater	Pullover
room	Zimmer; Platz	sixth	sechste(r; s)	sweet(s)	Süßigkeit(en)
rose	Rose	skate	Rollschuh fahren	swim	schwimmen
(newspaper) round	Zeitung austragen	ski	Ski fahren	swimming pool	Schwimmbecken
		skirt	Rock		
rub	reiben	slap	schlagen, klopfen	**T**	
rubber	Gummi; Radiergummi	sleep	schlafen	table	Tabelle; Tisch
rule	Regel; beherrschen	slow	langsam	tail	Schwanz
ruler	Lineal	small	klein	take	(mit)nehmen
run	laufen, rennen	smile	lächeln	take out	herausnehmen
running	Laufen, Rennen	smoke	Rauch	tale	Geschichte
		snake	Schlange	talk	sprechen, sich unterhalten
S		sneeze	niesen		
sad	traurig	snow	schneien	tall	hoch; groß
salad	Salat	snowmobile	Motorschlitten	tank	(Flüssigkeits)behälter; Tank; (Wasser)becken; hier: Aquarium
salt	Salz	so	so; also; damit		
the same	der-/die-/dasselbe	sock	Socke		
Saturday	Samstag	sofa	Sofa, Couch	tea	Tee
sauce	Soße	some	einige; etwas	teacher	Lehrer/in
save	retten	somebody	jemand	tear	Träne
saxophone	Saxophon	something	etwas	telephone	Telefon
say	sagen	sometimes	manchmal	television	Fernseher
scare	Angst machen, erchrecken	son	Sohn	tell	erzählen
		song	Lied	ten	zehn
be scared	Angst haben	soon	bald	tenth	zehnte(r; s)
scary	furchterregend; unheimlich	sorry	Verzeihung, Entschuldigung	terrible	schrecklich, furchtbar
				terror	schreckliche Angst
school	Schule	sound	Geräusch; Klang	text message	SMS
scissors (pl)	Schere	soup	Suppe	thank you	danke
scooter	Roller	Spanish	spanisch; Spanisch	thank you very much	vielen Dank
sea	Meer	speak	sprechen		
second	zweite(r; s)	special	besondere(r; s)	thanks	danke
see	sehen	spell	buchstabieren	that	das; der/die/das; dass
See you soon.	Bis bald.	spend	ausgeben (Geld); verbringen (Zeit)	the	der/die/das
sellotape	Klebestreifen			their	ihr(e)
send	senden	spider	Spinne	them	sie, ihnen
send in	einsenden, einreichen	spinach	Spinat	then	damals; dann
sentence	Satz	sport	Sport; Sportart	there	dort(hin)
September	September	sports	Sport-	there are	es gibt, da sind
servant	Diener/in				

there is	es gibt, da ist
these	diese
they	sie
thing	Ding, Gegenstand
think	denken, glauben, meinen
third	dritte(r, s)
thirsty	durstig
thirteen	dreizehn
thirteenth	dreizehnte(r, s)
thirtieth	dreißigste(r, s)
thirty-first	einunddreißigste(r; s)
this	diese(r, s)
this is	das ist
This is me.	Das bin ich.
those	diese; jene
thousand	Tausend
three	drei
thrilling	faszinierend, aufregend
throw	werfen
Thursday	Donnerstag
ticket	Eintrittskarte
tickle	kitzeln
tiger	Tiger
time	(Uhr)zeit; Mal
(three) times a day	drei Mal am Tag
tin	Büchse, Dose
tired	müde
to	zu, bis, vor
today	heute
together	zusammen, gemeinsam
tomato (pl tomatoes)	Tomate
tomorrow	morgen
tongue	Zunge
too	zu; auch
top	oberes Ende; hier: Spitze
tortoise	(Land)schildkröte
total	gesamt; Gesamt-
touch	berühren
towards	in Richtung, auf ... zu
tower	Turm
town	Stadt
toy	Spielzeug
trainer	Turnschuh
trap	Falle
treasure	Schatz
tree	Baum
trick (somebody)	jdm austricksen
trip	Ausflug, Reise
trouble	Schwierigkeiten, Ärger
trousers (no pl)	Hose
true	wahr
truth	Wahrheit
try	versuchen
Tuesday	Dienstag
turkey	Pute(r); Truthahn
turn	(sich) drehen; sich umdrehen
turn off	abschalten
turn on	einschalten
TV	Fernseher, Fernsehen
twelfth	zwölfte(r, s)
twelve	zwölf
twentieth	zwanzigste(r, s)
twenty	zwanzig
twenty-first	einundzwanzigste(r, s)
twenty-five	fünfundzwanzig
twenty-four	vierundzwanzig

twenty-fourth	vierundzwanzigste(r, s)
twenty-ninth	neunundzwanzigste(r, s)
twenty-one	einundzwanzig
twenty-second	zweiundzwanzigste(r, s)
twenty-third	dreiundzwanzigste(r, s)
twenty-three	dreiundzwanzig
twenty-two	zweiundzwanzig
twice	zweimal
twins	Zwillinge
two	zwei

U

umbrella	Regenschirm
under	unter
understand	verstehen
(the) United Kingdom (UK)	das Vereinigte Königreich (Großbritannien und Nordirland)
unhappy	unglücklich
universe	Universum
unusual	ungewöhnlich
upon	auf, an
us	uns
use	benutzen
usually	gewöhnlich, normalerweise

V

vegetable	Gemüse
very	sehr
village	Dorf
visit	besuchen

W

wait	warten
wait for	warten auf
wake up	aufwecken; aufwachen
walk	(zu Fuß) gehen
want	wünschen; wollen
warm	warm
washing machine	Waschmaschine
watch	Uhr; beobachten, zuschauen
watch TV	fernsehen
water	Wasser
watercolour	Wasserfarbe
wave	winken
we	wir
we're (we are)	wir sind
wear	tragen
weather	Wetter
Wednesday	Mittwoch
week	Woche
weekend	Wochenende
welcome	Willkommen!
well	nun (ja), tja
well done	gut gemacht
western	Western
what	was
What about ...	Was ist mit ...?
What a mess!	Was für eine Unordnung!
What a pity!	Schade!
What else?	Was noch?
What's going on?	Was ist los?
What's the matter?	Was ist los?
when	wann; wenn; als
where	wo(hin)
whisper	flüstern

white	weiß
who	wer
whole	ganz
why	warum
widescreen	Breitbild-
wife (pl wives)	Ehefrau
wiggle	wackeln (mit)
wild	wild
win	gewinnen
wind	Wind
window	Fenster
winter	Winter
wipe	abwischen, abputzen
wish	(sich) wünschen
with	mit, bei
wolf (pl wolves)	Wolf
wonderful	wunderbar; wundervoll
wood	Wald, Holz
wooden	Holz-, hölzern
woods	Wäldchen
word	Wort
work	arbeiten
world	Welt, Erde
worry	sich Sorgen machen
would	würde, würdest
write	schreiben
wrong	falsch

Y

year	Jahr
yellow	gelb
yes	ja
yesterday	gestern
yoghurt	Joghurt
you	du, dich, dir; Sie, Ihnen; ihr, euch
You're welcome.	Nichts zu danken. Keine Ursache. Gern geschehen.
young	jung
your	dein(e); euer/eure; Ihr(e)
yourself	du, dich, dir; selbst
yuck	igitt, pfui
yummy	lecker

Z

zoo	Zoo

Key

Plural nouns — irregular plurals

1 7, 1, 8, 11, 4, 2, 12, 9, 5, 3, 10, 6

2
1 a snake
2 three snakes
3 a laptop
4 five frogs
5 a ball
6 four ice creams
7 seven apples
8 five insects
9 two rabbits
10 a rabbit
11 two babies
12 six balls
13 two cows
14 twelve bananas
15 four fish
16 six children

3
1 dogs   6 hamsters
2 ponies   7 insects
3 cats   8 feet
4 babies   9 fish
5 mice   10 children

Imperatives

1
1 Sh. Don't speak.
2 Don't clean the board.
3 Sit down, please.
4 Open you bags, please.
5 Don't eat the banana.
6 Don't open the window.
7 Look at me.
8 Run!

2
1 Don't open the window.
2 Don't walk.
3 Don't close your books.
4 Don't stand up.
5 Don't look at the picture.
6 Don't tell me your name.
7 Don't speak.
8 Don't eat your apple.

3
1 Close the door.
2 Don't open your books.
3 Don't look at me.
4 Tell me your name.
5 Take your books out.
   (Or Take out your books.)
6 Don't clean the window.
7 Don't eat my ice cream.
8 Put your pen in your bag.

4
1 up   5 at me
2 down   6 the window
3 my chocolate   7 books
4 your name   8 green

5
1 Stand up.
2 Sit down.
3 Don't run.
4 Don't talk.
5 Open your books.
6 Clean the board.
7 Don't eat the cake.
8 Close the window.

to be (affirmative)

1
1 It's green.
2 They're twelve.
3 He's tired.
4 We're twelve.
5 I'm busy.
6 She's tired.
7 They're busy.
8 They're green.

2
1 am   2 is   3 is   4 are
5 are   6 is   7 are   8 are

Prepositions

1
1 F   2 F   3 T   4 T
5 T   6 T   7 F   8 F

2
1 on   4 in   7 under
2 next to   5 in   8 next to
3 under   6 on

there is / there are

1
1 g   2 d   3 c   4 f
5 b   6 a   7 h   8 e

2
1 are   2 's   3 's   4 are
5 's   6 are   7 's   8 's / are

3
1 There are two dogs on the table.
2 There's a bear in the bag.
3 There are four gorillas next to the bed.
4 There are three bears in the car.
5 There's a dog under the chair.
6 There's a gorilla in the fridge.

4
1 There's an insect in it.
2 There are three frogs
3 There's a snake under the
4 There's a gorilla in
5 There's a cat on
6 There are two bears

have got — haven't got

1
1 T   2 F   3 T   4 F
5 T   6 F   7 F   8 F

2
1 Maggie   2 Susan
3 Louise   4 Annabel

3
1 We've got a new car.
2 My mother has got blue eyes.
3 I have got six brothers and sisters.
4 A snake hasn't got legs.
5 We haven't got homework tonight.
6 My family hasn't got a dog.

4
1 I haven't got long hair.
2 They haven't got green eyes.
3 My father hasn't got a big car.
4 She hasn't got a new laptop.
5 I haven't got homework this weekend.
6 We haven't got a dog.

5
1 A *Have* you *got* a cat?
   B No, but I've got a dog!
2 A *Has* your brother *got* a big nose?
   B No, but he *has got / 's got* big ears!
3 A *Have* your parents *got* a car?
   B Yes, and my sister *has got / 's got* a car, too.
4 A *Has* your classroom *got* a computer?
   B No, but the school *has got / 's got* a special computer room.
5 A *Have* you *got* a laptop?
   B No, I *haven't / have not*!

6
1 've got   7 hasn't got
2 has got   8 have got
3 has got   9 has got
4 hasn't got   10 has got
5 has got   11 haven't got
6 has got

to be (negative)

1
1 English   2 grey   3 wrong
4 hot   5 morning   6 small

2
1 Today isn't Tuesday.
2 The cat isn't under the chair.
3 Charlotte isn't happy.
4 The pens aren't on the book.
5 It isn't morning.
6 The frog isn't on the crocodile.

3
1 She isn't Italian.
2 They aren't happy.
3 I'm not bored.
4 We aren't cold.

4
1 I'm not English.
2 You aren't 15.
3 They aren't French.
4 He isn't happy.
5 We aren't from Genova.
6 It isn't blue.

5
1 'm not   2 'm not   3 aren't
4 isn't   5 aren't

6
1 T
2 F — Peter and Paul aren't pelicans. They're owls.
3 F — Lumpy isn't a hippo. He's a camel.
4 F — Henry isn't an elephant. He's a hippo.
5 T
6 F — Kate and Andre aren't hamsters. They're monkeys.
7 F — Daisy isn't an owl. She's a hamster.
8 F — Rio isn't a mouse. He's an elephant.
9 T

Questions with *be*

1
1 No, he isn't.
2 Yes, she is.
3 No, it isn't.
4 Yes, they are.
5 Yes, you are.
6 Yes, I am.

2
1 Are
2 Am
3 Are
4 Is
5 Are
6 Is
7 Are
8 Is

3
1 A *Is* it her birthday?
   B Yes, it *is*.
2 A *Are* you angry?
   B Yes, I *am*.
3 A *Is* your computer new?
   B No, it *isn't*.
4 A *Am* I wrong?
   B Yes, you *are*.
5 A *Are* the children hungry?
   B No, they *aren't*.
6 A *Are* we late?
   B Yes, we *are*.
7 A *Is* Carl scared?
   B No, he *isn't*.
8 A *Is* Jane your friend?
   B Yes, she *is*.

4
1 Are you 12 today?
2 Am I late for school?
3 Are your eyes blue?
4 Is Julia your best friend?
5 Is the book under the table?
6 Is Dave from Australia?
7 Are we busy this weekend?

5
1 6   2 3   3 1   4 2
5 7   6 4   7 5

6
1 No, he isn't.
2 Yes, it is.
3 No, it isn't.
4 No, they aren't.
5 Yes, they are.
6 No, it isn't.
7 No, they aren't.
8 Yes, it is.

Possessives

1
1 my   7 Her   13 My
2 I   8 He   14 We
3 their   9 His   15 their
4 Our   10 It's   16 our
5 Its   11 Their   17 My
6 She   12 they

2
1 my   4 their
2 her   5 your
3 his   6 Its

3
1 my / Her   2 His
3 their   4 its

can – can't

1
a Liam   e Oliver
b Paul   f Jack
c Sue   g Claire
d Janice   h Kylie

2
1 I can't climb the tree.
2 I can't eat ice-cream.
3 I can't speak.
4 I can't walk.
5 I can't eat pizza.
6 I can't play my computer game.

3
1 Can you swim?
2 Can you speak French?
3 Can your father speak English?
4 Can you ride a horse?
5 Can you walk on your hands?
6 Can you play the guitar?
7 Can you stand on your head?
8 Can you say the names of ten English cities?

Present simple

1

```
R W A I T E S N T A E S
A A R R I V B U Y R F H
N T I S I R E R A R W U
S C L I M E R T H I F O
E H E A B R E K O V A P
R B K A E R B U T E L E
G R H E A R S N Y A L P
O A W A T C M I O P L R
T L A C L I M B L O E I
H E Q U I E R S A B E D
A D E G V O S W I T C H
H E L P E A B N M O P E
```

2
1 watch   5 goes
2 likes   6 climbs
3 love   7 go
4 buy   8 plays

3
plays, arrives, climbs, leaves, falls, goes, carries, watches

4
1 leaves   8 sit
2 goes   9 wait
3 watches   10 arrives
4 see   11 hits
5 runs   12 run
6 climbs   13 picks
7 sits   14 go

5
1 play   5 carry
2 plays   6 carries
3 wash   7 goes
4 washes   8 go

6 c, e, a, f, d, b

7
1 goes   9 looks
2 leaves   10 jumps
3 walks   11 runs
4 loves   12 walks
5 go   13 goes
6 buys   14 picks
7 leaves   15 carries
8 stops

8
1 watches   9 sits
2 gets up   10 looks
3 eats   11 waits
4 takes   12 arrives
5 leaves   13 writes
6 walks   14 goes
7 goes   15 likes
8 climbs

Possessive *'s*

1
1 My brother's   5 The teacher's
2 My mother   6 Sally's
3 My father's   7 Sally
4 My sister   8 Paul's

2
1 My mother's favourite food is spaghetti.
2 Sally's favourite book is Harry Potter.
3 The teacher's favourite sentence is 'Be quiet'.
4 My father's favourite word is 'No'.
5 Tom's favourite sport is tennis.
6 Steve's favourite day of the week is Sunday.
7 Betty's favourite food is honey.
8 My sister's favourite day of the week is Friday.

Articles a – an

1
1 a	2 a	3 a
4 an	5 a	6 a
7 an	8 a	9 an

2 In the fridge I can see

an	old shoe onion apple egg	and a	carrot potato pepper mango frog

3
1 a	6 an	11 a
2 a	7 an	12 an
3 a	8 a	13 a
4 a	9 a	14 an
5 an	10 a	15 an

Present simple negative

1
| 1 d | 2 f | 3 h | 4 a |
| 5 e | 6 b | 7 g | 8 c |

2
1 Jack doesn't play guitar in my band.
2 My brothers don't speak French.
3 I don't love Aaron.
4 Sally doesn't like lots of vegetables.
5 We don't play tennis every day.
6 My dog doesn't like cats.
7 They don't walk to school.
8 Dad doesn't read the newspaper in the mornings.

3
1 don't eat spinach
2 doesn't play drums
3 doesn't play volleyball
4 don't like mornings
5 don't speak German
6 don't like red
7 don't read newspapers
8 don't ride horses

4
1 doesn't like	7 doesn't eat
2 likes	8 eats
3 doesn't eat	9 lives
4 eats	10 doesn't live
5 lives	11 doesn't like
6 doesn't live	12 likes

5
1 live	13 look
2 doesn't live	14 drives
3 loves	15 takes
4 plays	16 cooks
5 watches	17 cleans
6 doesn't like	18 don't help
7 loves	19 sit
8 goes	20 watch
9 doesn't watch	21 doesn't see
10 meets	22 falls
11 go	23 don't know
12 don't buy	

Adverbs of frequency

1
| 1 T | 2 F | 3 F | 4 T |
| 5 T | 6 F | 7 T | 8 F |

2
1 often	5 always
2 sometimes	6 usually
3 never	7 never
4 often	8 often

3
1 am I happy always – I'm always happy.
2 I never do homework.
3 My mum usually cooks pizza for dinner.
4 We sometimes have ice cream too.
5 I sometimes go shopping after school.
6 My friends and I often play football.
7 We are never bored.
8 We are always excited about the weekend.

4
1 ✗ – On Mondays, she often goes shopping.
2 ✓
3 ✗ – On Wednesdays, she is always hot.
4 ✗ – On Thursdays, she usually sees her friends.
5 ✓
6 ✓
7 ✗ – On Sundays, she often eats in the best restaurant.
8 ✗ – She is always bored.

5
1 I'm never late to school.
2 Dad often watches TV in the evenings.
3 The children are sometimes tired after school.
4 We always wash the car Sunday.
5 She's usually bored at the weekend.
6 My sister never eats carrots.
7 I usually do my homework before dinner.
8 It's always cold in December.

Present simple questions & short answers

1
1 Does	2 Do	3 Does
4 Do	5 Does	6 Do
7 Does	8 Do	

2
| 1 e | 2 g | 3 h | 4 a |
| 5 b | 6 c | 7 d | 8 f |

3
1 No, I don't.
2 Yes, she does.
3 Yes, he does.
4 No, they don't.
5 Yes, I do.
6 No, she doesn't.
7 Yes, they do.
8 No, she doesn't.

4
1 Do	6 do
2 don't	7 Does
3 Does	8 doesn't
4 does	9 Does
5 Do	10 doesn't

5
1 Q Does Ricky Starr drive a nice car?
  A Yes, he does.
2 Q Does Ricky Starr wear a silly hat?
  A No, he doesn't.
3 Q Does Ricky Starr wear shoes?
  A No, he doesn't.
4 Q Does Ricky Starr speak French?
  A Yes, he does.
5 Q Do they want Ricky Starr's autograph?
  A Yes, they do.
6 Q Do they like Ricky Starr?
  A Yes, they do.
7 Q Do they like Ricky Starr?
  A No, they don't.
8 Q Is Ricky Starr happy?
  A No, he isn't.

6
1 Do you like opera?
2 Do you eat meat?
3 Do you wear red clothes?
4 Do you play tennis?
5 Does your father cook?
6 Does your best friend speak English?
7 Do all your friends go to the same school?
8 Does your headmaster know your name?

Question words

1
1 What is your name?
2 Where do you live?
3 How often do you come here?
4 What do hamsters eat?
5 How often do you go to the cinema?
6 Where do you keep your pet snake?

2
1 How		5 Where	
2 What's		6 How often	
3 Where		7 What	
4 What		8 How often	

Object pronouns

1
1 them	2 it	3 him
4 you	5 it	6 her
7 us	8 them	

2
1 me	2 her	3 them
4 it	5 him	6 me
7 him	8 them	9 us

this, that / these, those

1
1 Do you like these goldfish?
2 I want that fish over there.
3 Would you like this lollipop?
4 No, I'd like that lollipop over there.
5 I think these shoes are too big.
6 OK, can we try those shoes, over there?
7 I think this apple is a bit old.
8 OK, try one of those apples.

2
1 those	2 that	3 this
4 That	5 these	6 those
7 these	8 that	

3
1 this	2 that	3 these
4 those	5 this	6 those
7 that	8 These	

How much is/are...?

1
1 are	2 is		3 is		4 are
5 are	6 is		7 are		8 is

2
1 are	5 are	9 are	13 are
2 are	6 is	10 is	14 is
3 is	7 is	11 is	
4 is	8 are	12 is	

3
How much are the scissors?
— They're £1.90.
How much is the exercise book? — It's £2.40.
How much is the pencil case? — It's £4.
How much is the ruler? — It's £1.20.
How much are the pens? — They're £1.50.
How much are the pencils? — They're £1.
How much are the rubbers? — They're £2.
How much is the pencil sharpener? — It's £1.

Present continuous

1
1 Gillie watching a DVD.
2 Someone is knocking on the window.
3 Gillie calling her dad.
4 Dad having a shower.
5 Gillie walking to the window.
6 There's mum — she's looking for her key!

2
1 gymnastics
2 a karate suit
3 a picture in a book
4 karate
5 playing football
6 are dancing
7 he doing
8 doing a sport
9 He's trying

3
1 aren't	4 aren't	7 Are
2 not	5 Is	8 talking
3 enjoying	6 aren't	

4
1 We aren't watching TV.
2 They aren't swimming.
3 I'm not keeping fit at the moment.
4 Susan isn't learning karate.
5 Jane and Tim aren't trying to do their homework.
6 John isn't playing tennis with his friend.
7 I'm not listening to my CDs.
8 They aren't singing a song.

5
1 Are / am	5 Is / is
2 Is / isn't	6 Are / aren't
3 Is / isn't	7 Am / are
4 Are / 'm not	8 Are / are

6
1 're / are	5 'm / am	9 's / is
2 's / is	6 'm / am	10 's / is
3 's / is	7 'm / am	11 are
4 am	8 're / are	12 're/are

7
1 He's playing
2 They are / they're listening
3 He is / He's watching
4 I'm / I am doing
5 I'm / I am not doing
6 She is / She's riding
7 It isn't / It is not raining.
8 she isn't / is not listening

8
1 's ringing / 'm watching
2 writes / 's writing
3 's going / 's travelling
4 go / buy
5 go / goes
6 reads / 's reading
7 are dancing / 're having
8 are playing / doesn't like / isn't playing

9
1 come	8 're buying
2 stay	9 have
3 don't enjoy	10 's talking
4 's raining	11 lives
5 'm sitting	12 likes
6 'm writing	13 's shouting
7 're doing	14 's laughing

10
1 lives
2 's / is playing
3 Do / play / sing
4 'm / am doing
5 Are / watching
6 wears

11
1 are you going	5 Do / play
2 do	6 am / 'm learning
3 Do / wear	7 goes
4 know	

Ordinal numbers

1

A	S	E	C	O	N	D	S	T
T	W	E	L	F	T	H	L	W
H	T	E	P	O	E	S	E	E
R	H	C	O	R	I	E	C	N
F	I	R	S	T	T	V	R	T
I	R	G	I	H	G	E	T	I
F	D	I	X	T	H	N	H	E
T	E	N	T	E	N	T	H	T
H	I	X	H	H	A	H	O	H

78

2 1 d 2 f 3 a 4 e
5 g 6 c 7 h 8 b

3 6, six, 6th, sixth
2, two, 2nd, second
21, twenty-one, 21st, twenty-first
17, seventeen, 17th, seventeenth
5, five, 5th, fifth
3, three, 3rd, third
70, seventy, 70th, seventieth
44, forty-four, 44th, forty-forth

4 1 second   4 ninth
2 fifth   5 sixth, seventh
3 January   6 sixth, eighth

Time prepositions

1 1 at   2 at   3 on
4 on   5 at   6 in
7 on   8 On, in   9 on
10 at   11 in   12 at, at

2 1 on   2 on   3 on
4 at   5 in   6 at
7 on   8 at   9 at
10 in   11 in   12 at
13 at   14 on

Past simple — *was / were*

1 a Sturday   d Friday
b Thursday   e Wednesday
c Monday   f Tuesday

2 1 Ben was in bed.
2 June and Simon were on the farm.
3 Mrs Gladstone was in the garden.
4 Kevin and Lucy were at school.
5 Mr Thomas was at the cinema.
6 May and Annabel were on a pond.
7 Liam and Fred were at a concert.
8 Tina was in a field.

3 1 No, he wasn't.
2 Yes, they were.
3 No, she wasn't.
4 Yes, they were.
5 Yes, he was.
6 No, they weren't.
7 No, they weren't.
8 Yes, she was.

4 1 was   11 was   21 were
2 was   12 wasn't   22 was
3 was   13 was   23 were
4 were   14 Was   24 were
5 was   15 was   25 were
6 were   16 was   26 was
7 were   17 weren't   27 was
8 wasn't   18 was   28 wasn't
9 wasn't   19 were   29 was
10 was   20 weren't

5 1 I wasn't happy yesterday.
2 Nigel wasn't hungry after the walk.
3 Mum and dad weren't at my school this morning.
4 They weren't excited about my birthday.
5 We weren't ill after the meal in that restaurant
6 I wasn't at home yesterday at 6 pm.
7 It wasn't very hot in Spain for our holidays.
8 The party wasn't excellent.

6 1 were   10 were
2 wasn't   11 weren't
3 were   12 was
4 were   13 was
5 was   14 were
6 was   15 was
7 Was   16 was
8 was   17 wasn't
9 was   18 was

7 1 Were you bored yesterday?
2 Where were you at 8 p.m. yesterday?
3 Who were you with on Sunday afternoon?
4 Where were you at 8 a.m. this morning?
5 Was your best friend happy yesterday?
6 Were you at school yesterday afternoon?

Past simple — regular verbs

1 1 f   2 j   3 b   4 g   5 a
6 i   7 c   8 h   9 e   10 d

2 1 phone, phoned
2 walk, walked
3 plays, played
4 carries, carried
5 study, studied
6 chased, chases
7 interview, interviewed
8 asked, asks

3 1 studied   9 pushed
2 wanted   10 chased
3 walked   11 phoned
4 started   12 arrived
5 stopped   13 asked
6 jumped   14 happened
7 shouted   15 looked
8 tried   16 laughed

Past simple — irregular verbs

1 1 went   4 put   7 held
2 sat   5 told   8 had
3 ate   6 said

2 regular

verb	past form
follow	followed
change	changed
carry	carried
notice	noticed
push	pushed
try	tried
wait	waited
stop	stopped

irregular

verb	past form
leave	left
do	did
know	knew
give	gave
eat	ate
take	took
put	put
see	saw

3 1 rang   5 told   9 gave
2 heard   6 left   10 ran
3 was   7 went
4 had   8 met

4 put, held, said, saw, was, carried, sat, took

5 1 held   5 took
2 carried   6 saw
3 put   7 was
4 sat   8 said

6 a 10 a.m.   c 6 p.m.
b 11 a.m.   d 8 p.m.

7 1 had   5 left
2 ran   6 did
3 ate   7 went
4 met

8 1 followed   17 noticed
2 was   18 did
3 hurried   19 got
4 ran   20 got
5 opened   21 sat
6 walked   22 sat
7 started   23 waved
8 was   24 waved

9	was	25	knew
10	was	26	was
11	made	27	turned
12	sat	28	watched
13	turned	29	saw
14	changed	30	heard
15	was	31	turned
16	took	32	was

9 Jack ran to his front door.
It was warm inside.
Jack made a cup of coffee.
Jack changed channels.
Jack waved at the man on the TV.
Someone made a noise in the house.
Jack was happy to be home.
Someone was in the house.
Someone followed Jack home.
Jack sat on the sofa.
Jack turned off the TV.
It was cold outside.

Linking words (and, but, because)

1
1	e	2	a	3	d	4	h
5	b	6	f	7	c	8	g

2
1	e	2	a	3	f
4	b	5	d	6	c

3
1	because	5	and
2	and	6	but
3	because	7	because
4	because	8	and

4
1 and, but, because
2 and, because, but
3 because, and, but
4 because, and, but
5 and, but, because
6 but, and, because
7 and, but, because
8 but, and, because

5
1	because	8	and
2	but	9	because
3	because	10	but
4	and	11	and
5	but	12	and
6	because	13	and
7	But	14	and

Past simple – negation with did

1
1	past	5	past
2	past	6	present
3	present	7	past
4	present	8	past

2
1 The cat didn't like the milk.
2 He didn't eat his peas.
3 He had a bad dream.
4 He rescued us.
5 He didn't think it was funny.
6 He caught the ball.
7 She didn't go to school today.
8 She enjoyed the party.

3
1	like	5	sit
2	have	6	like
3	talk	7	know
4	dance	8	stay

4
1 I fed the cat.
2 I did my homework.
3 I ate my dinner.
4 I wore my hat.
5 I cleaned my bike.
6 I helped my mother.
7 I walked the dog.
8 I played with my brother.

5
1	didn't take	5	didn't hear
2	didn't go	6	didn't see
3	didn't ring	7	didn't notice
4	didn't stop	8	didn't ride

6
1	g	2	d	3	f	4	a
5	e	6	b	7	h	8	c

7
1	Were you	6	didn't see
2	didn't go	7	I didn't know
3	didn't look	8	I didn't
4	you didn't	9	bought
5	didn't read	10	bought you

8
1	didn't like	5	didn't say
2	didn't invite	6	didn't watch
3	didn't see	7	didn't go
4	didn't enjoy	8	didn't eat

9
1	didn't know	5	didn't sleep
2	didn't watch	6	didn't eat
3	didn't want	7	didn't help
4	didn't ring	8	didn't buy

10
1	found	7	looked
2	asked	8	didn't find
3	didn't hear	9	dropped
4	spoke	10	lost
5	heard	11	asked
6	offered	12	told

11
1	decided	10	saw
2	dug	11	shouted
3	put	12	said
4	didn't like		
5	asked		
6	didn't understand		
7	didn't clean		
8	didn't want		
9	arrived		

(be) going to

1
1	g	2	e	3	b	4	a	5	i
6	h	7	f	8	d	9	c	10	j

2
1	F	2	F	3	T	4	T
5	F	6	T	7	F	8	F

3
1	'm going to	6	are going to
2	Are … going to	7	is going to
		8	are, going to
3	are going to	9	is going to
4	is going to	10	are, going to
5	are, going to	11	am going to

4
1 A What are you going to do tomorrow?
B I'm going to wash my dad's car.
2 A Are you going to play football with us?
B No, I'm going to visit my aunt and uncle.
3 A Are you going to watch a DVD?
B Yes, I'm going to watch my favourite film.
4 A Are your parents going to give you a bicycle for your birthday?
B No, they're going to give me a new laptop.
5 A What are you going to do on Sunday?
B We're going to swim in the river.

5
1 John's going to write an email.
2 Pauline is going to climb a tree.
3 Gran is going to drink a cup of tea.
4 Tommy and Angie are going to cook spaghetti.
5 The dog is going to swim in the river.
6 We are going to play football.

6
1 are going to visit
2 are going to stay
3 am going to listen
4 are … going to do
5 am going to think
6 is going to watch
7 are going to come
8 am going to cook
9 are going to eat

7
1 He's going to clean his bicycle.
2 She's going to play tennis.
3 They are going to learn French.
4 They are going to fly to London.
5 It is going to catch the bird.